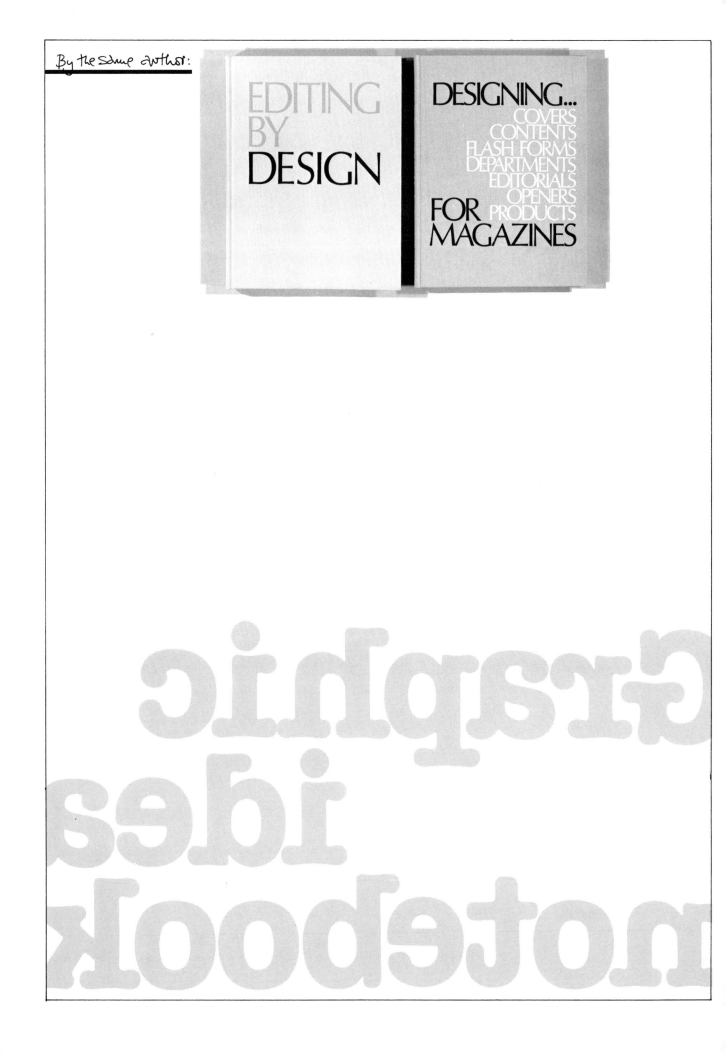

Jan V. White

Graphic idea

Inventive techniques for designing printed pages

idea

notebook

WATSON-GUPTILL PUBLICATIONS, New York

Copyright ©1980 by Jan White

First published 1980 in the United States and Canada by Watson-Guptill Publications,
a division of Billboard Publications, Inc.,
1515 Broadway, New York, N.Y. 10036

Library of Congress Cataloging in Publication Data

White, Jan V   1928–
    Graphic idea notebook.

    Includes index.
    1. Printing, Practical—Layout. 2. Graphic arts.
3. Pictures—Printing. I. Title.
Z246.W58   1980   686.2′24   80–423
ISBN 0–8230–2149–1

Manufactured in U.S.A.

First Printing, 1980
5   6   7   8   9/86   85

A few words about word-people and "Art":

Editors are inevitably overworked, short-handed, underfinanced, and behind schedule. That is simply part of the definition of "editor." But, much more serious, editors of all varieties of publications—magazines, newspapers, books, newsletters, house organs; cheap or expensive, flossy or plain—are also fundamentally word-oriented.

For many editors, "art" is secondary, after-the-fact, and something that has to be grudgingly accepted as an unavoidable nuisance, necessary for "dressing up" the pages. An editor may be a former English major, or an ex-engineer who gravitated to the magazine of his or her specialty, or a newspaper-oriented journalism graduate who sees pictures as sidebars, or maybe just a generalist who somehow got stuck with the company periodical. As such, all of them are experts when it comes to knowing what the story is about, understanding its content and gauging its potential effect on their audience. They are eminently qualified to make judgments about these things.

They also *know what they like* in terms of "design" when they see it somewhere else. But they are too often unable to combine these insights: that is, to give form (i.e. "design") to those precious words. They are stumped because they must deal with what they fear as "art." So they pass the buck to the art department (or whatever version of art help is available) or if they are do-it-yourselfers, they most probably put off thinking about it until the last possible moment.

Many editors feel hamstrung by their lack of expertise in "art"; they are daunted by their unfamiliarity with the jargon; and they are worried by their admitted incapacity to draw a straight line (which seems to be the standard excuse not to try). Many of them are so needlessly intimidated by their lack of knowledge about graphic design that they don't see the simple truth: ninety-nine percent of what is called "art" or "design" in publishing is really nothing but common sense. It is simply the graphic expression of the content of the story. It is just taking a bunch of thoughts and giving them visible form in type, in illustrative images of some sort, and in the arrangement of those elements on the page.

Publication design is not an arcane, occult, esoteric skill. There is no secret password or handshake to get into the club. Page design is merely the last step of the editing process.

All that editors need to do is broaden their view to include that extra dimension their stories take when they are metamorphosed from manuscript into printed page form. Obviously, there must be a natural relationship between the direction of a story's thoughts and the appearance of those thoughts in print. That relationship must be simple, clear, and appropriate. It is successful only when it is editorially logical. And logic is another word for common sense—a commodity that word-people have plenty of.

now a few words about picture-people:

Designers, like editors, are overworked, short-handed, and underfinanced. They are even farther behind schedule than editors because they get squeezed between editorial delays and unextendable publishing deadlines. Too often they are asked to be brilliant and creative under the gun, thinking up clever concepts on the one hand, and solving jigsaw puzzles on the other—both on the spur of the moment. To complicate matters, seldom if ever do the editors help them by explaining the purpose of the story so they can bring it out and give it visibility through expressive handling of the material on the page. Most likely, the editors don't realize how essential such an understanding is and how much better the result could be if the designer had it!

As a result, the designers' job remains limited to making handsome page arrangements for the sake of making handsome page arrangements. Prettification.

Frankly, such prettification is indeed that arcane mystery editors believe it to be, because it is based on subjective "liking" by the designer. But good publication design is far more functional and important than just that. Given half a chance to base his work on an understanding of the journalism involved, the designer can be of tremendous help to the editors in producing a piece that *communicates* while looking pretty. Looking pretty is a by-product: the prime purpose of an art director's work is to apply his or her knowledge of design techniques to catapult ideas off the page into the reader's mind.

This implies an understanding of both editorial purposes and graphic techniques, to make sure that the graphic techniques that are chosen are the right ones for the job, for editorial reasons and not artistic reasons: for reasons that are significant and justified by the contents of the story. That is why understanding the purpose of the story is the first essential for the designer. And that is why designers have to add journalistic ambition to their artistic ambition and get their kicks from achieving a well-communicated message rather than from devising a stunning layout.

about the team of word-people and picture-people:

Editors and designers must work together as a team. To function optimally they should keep two very important factors in mind:

1/ There's nothing new under the sun. Someone somewhere thought up the same idea or used the same trick. There is no point in trying to reinvent the wheel. All that is needed is to use common sense and intelligence in order to turn the same old tried-and-true materials into a fresh and unexpected mix. Such a new mix may well turn out to be clever and innovative, even original. Wonderful! But that's just gravy. Originality per se is not the purpose of the exercise. The true purpose is to make dull material interesting, thus to catch the reader's attention, hold it, and transmit a message. To do this successfully means that we must make the most of those special qualities that are inherent in the material, be they thoughts, facts, words, images, charts, tables, diagrams or whatnot. We must bring those qualities out and give them unmistakable visibility, so they can do their attention-attracting and story-telling.

2/ The vast majority of raw material we are faced with using in our publications is just plain dull. Most of it is repetition of, or (if we're lucky) variation on the same old themes whose importance lies in the information they contain. There's nothing wrong with that prosaic dullness. On the contrary: it provides an opportunity for editors and designers to become alchemists who transmute the dross into editorial gold.

Needed are: imagination; ingenuity; courage; time; effort; and some investment of treasure of course. But above all, what is needed is clear editing: a lucid understanding of what the point of all the material is—*the reason for publishing*. Once that is articulated, it can be given visibility and emphasis by graphics. In fact, GRAPHICS=EDITORIAL TOOL. That is the secret formula. Like all such "secrets" it is both obvious and deceptively simple.

and about this book:

It is a compendium of answers to various kinds of needs. When it was first conceived, (and when its first few pages were published in FOLIO magazine), it was entitled somewhat bombastically the *Editor's Vademecum*. I used the Latin because there seems to be no English equivalent to the concept of *vademecum*, which literally means "go with me." In English, the term refers to a ready reference book or manual that is *regularly* carried about by a person: a working companion. This is exactly what the *Graphic Idea Notebook* is intended to be—and it does this by fulfilling several functions.

Its fundamental purpose is to act as a SPARKPLUG FOR IDEAS, to jolt editors and art directors out of the habit patterns of thinking and working that we all fall into. We develop these habits as shortcuts for getting the job done as expediently as possible, but they can often become substitutes for original thinking and prevent us from seeing acutely, and solving problems inventively. This book is designed to be thumbed through when you need a new approach to handling some graphic dilemma. When the book is used in this general way, the fact that it is organized in categories can become a hindrance. So forget the arbitrary division of the subject matter in this case, and just riffle through the pages—the nub of the idea you need may well lie concealed where you might not expect it.

One important plea: don't get lost in the specifics of the illustrations. They are just "dummy" images to illustrate underlying principles. Avoid getting locked into thinking that the principle—as shown, perhaps, by an upside-down cow on page 15—can only be legitimately used for cows. It has validity for upside-down *anythings*; it is the upside-down-ness that matters, not the silly cow.

Most editors (and certainly all art directors) establish a secret file into which they stuff tearsheets of good ideas. Needless to say, these ideas are seldom properly filed. It usually follows that when an idea is needed in a hurry (meaning, of course, whenever one is needed), it cannot be found. What is usually found is a cache of oddments whose significance you cannot for the life of you recall. For frustrating years I dug through such a drawerful myself until, in desperation, I organized all the material according to problems-and-their-solutions: how to make things look old; how to show the passage of time; how to indicate improvement in value; how to symbolize ethnicity, and so forth. That was the foundation of this book, which is organized along the same lines.

Inclusion of material was based on three rational criteria: 1) Usefulness to the working editor and designer; 2) ease of production (cheapness); and 3) simplicity of explanation to suppliers and printers. So this book is a PRACTICAL GUIDE to what ought to be realistically feasible without too much stress on either patience or budget. And this brings us to another of the book's basic purposes.

How often do you remember some effective graphic technique you saw somewhere—yet you cannot remember exactly what it looked like, let alone where you saw it? But you know that it would be just right for this particular situation. It's nearly impossible to communicate this kind of half-recalled, undefined image to someone else without an example to show them. This book is arranged as a catalog precisely to help you deal with situations like this. If one of the illustrations can jog the memory of a specific technique you once saw, then it can be used as a SHOW-AND-TELL DOCUMENT to point to as you say, "Let's try something like this."

Since the book is organized around problems commonly faced in daily publishing practice, it also functions as a QUICK REFERENCE AID to help the enlightened editor or designer who is searching for that one special technique for dealing with a particular situation: how to make the most of a box, if that's all there is to work with; what to do with that bunch of uninspiring mugshots so they don't look like the ones in last month's issue; how to break up the text to turn it from a field of monolithic, daunting grey, into apparently shorter and easier-to-tackle chunks; how to bring out the hidden qualities in photos that are editorially significant but photographically dull—and so forth.

By the way, please note that the design of *The Graphic Idea Notebook* is itself a DEMONSTRATION of some of the graphic possibilities of our medium. The chapter openers all illustrate the three-dimensionality of a piece of paper—their purpose is to show that the flow of space from one side of the paper overleaf to the other can well be utilized for editorial purposes.

The cover, half-title, and title pages are also intended to be examples of this three-dimensionality. The positive front cover contrasted with the negative-and-backwards back cover illustrates the object-ness of the book; its "thing-ness." The half-title and title pages show the possibilities of making opaque paper appear to be transparent by printing identical images on both sides of the sheet, with the verso flopped, of course. What is it meant to prove? Who knows? But isn't it interesting?

The titles to some of the chapters are placed at peculiar angles. Why? As a reminder that everything need not be imposed in the available space in the expected vertical/horizontal relationship to the page's edges.

While on the subject of chapter openers, the pages opposite the chapter titles have been left blank expressly for the purpose of giving you space to annotate cross-references to your own material. As the "notebook" sits on the shelf above your desk and as you keep adding notes to it, it will become an increasingly useful PERSONAL SWIPEFILE. That's why I wrote the notes in it by hand rather than having them set in formal typography; I wanted to establish an informal atmosphere to encourage your own scribbling in it.

Now, as far as the irreverent bits of humor are concerned: they, too, are here for a serious purpose—to serve as a reminder not to take ourselves too seriously. Obviously, we try to make everything we publish as worthy, useful, and valuable as possible. But let's not forget that any single impression on a page is just one of a sequence of impressions in the publication as a whole, and that the next issue (next week, next month) will displace everything in the current one with a completely new set of such impressions. So how much does it really matter if we try a graphic trick and it falls flat (in our own hypercritical eyes)? There's always the next issue, so let us see our work in its full context, and take it with a pinch of salt or a grain of humor.

In no way does this imply that what editors and designers do is unimportant! The total image we build through our publications—in both their journalistic and graphic aspects—is desperately important. But any single detail must always be perceived as just that: a small part of a larger whole. To a great extent, this book is about DETAILING, and it is in the details that we can give free rein to our sense of humor and our desire to play. That is, after all, how we can make the product more lively. So let us risk failure in such a good cause, and if we don't create perfection every time, who cares?

There is no editor-in-chief in the sky keeping score!

It is customary to thank the people who have been helpful in the process of book-making. How I wish I could have palmed off some of the labors onto someone else! Alas, this book being the personal document it is, I was stuck with doing it all, even typing the damned manuscript. That's why there is so little text. But I must mention my dear wife, Clare, whose patience with ruined weekends ("I've got to get on with the *Notebook*, I can't go to the beach") was Job-like, and whose encouragement and support made it all possible.

And I must thank my friends Joe Hanson, Howard Ravis, and Chuck Tannen of FOLIO Magazine, who published many of these pages during the past three years. I do not thank them merely for the space they gave me—though that in itself ought to be enough—but because they ran the pages as delivered. Can you imagine? No editing! What luxury! What fun!

Westport, December 1979

Graphic Idea Notebook

Table of contents

Graphic Idea Notebook

Getting attention

HOW TO GET THE READER'S ATTENTION

The essential ingredient: a good editorial idea—one that is worth calling attention to. Without such value, no amount of graphic flamboyance makes sense. It may work that first time, and it may well yield some visual excitement for the issue. But that's cheating the reader who will grow suspicious of hype. And the magazine will suffer in the long run because of this inflation of presentation techniques.

BUT, if there is something worth trumpeting out loud, here is a collection of ways to do it (besides, of course, the fundamental way of making it big). Below: two useful attention-getting devices: 1) pinning the idea on someone the reader is likely to recognize and respect (Messrs. Napoleon, Beethoven and Shakespeare might fill the requirements?) and 2) elaborating the idea with symbols the reader recognizes as importance symbols (big exclamation points, out-of-scale quote marks, fat balloons). More on the pages that follow.

Smile -- tomorrow will be worse **!**

" Nothing is as easy as it looks **"**

Everything takes longer than you think

Simplify: edit out the competition. Get rid of the distractions, so the viewer is forced to pay attention to the elements that are editorially essential (ie. the reason for publishing).

The principle: NOTHING SUCCEEDS LIKE EXCESS

The practice: above: a frightening image. A fly isn't scary unless you perceive it as a threatening presence. What makes it so? Obviously: hugeness. (Normal sized flies are squashable). What makes the hugeness believable? The DETAILS which under normal viewing conditions would be invisible. Yecch!

Left: frightening images both. Skeletons are symbols of death... and muscle diagrams are just plain unappetizing

If we had second color available, you would see right away that Bessie is, in fact, bright PURPLE. Gilding the lily (or, here, purpling the cow) is an aspect of excess that also makes you look.

14

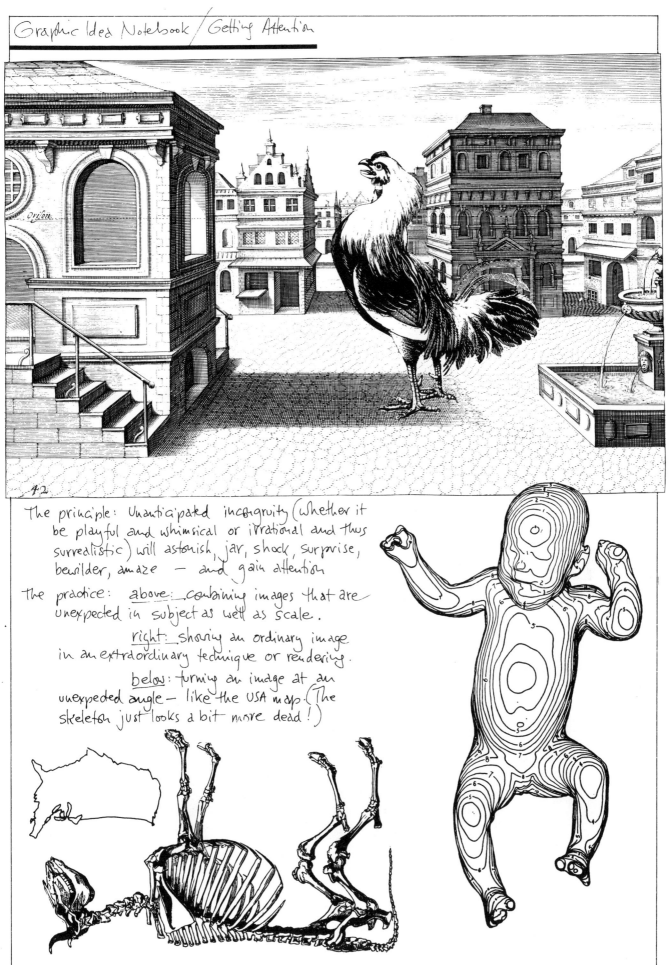

The principle: Unanticipated incongruity (whether it be playful and whimsical or irrational and thus surrealistic) will astonish, jar, shock, surprise, bewilder, amaze — and gain attention

The practice: above: combining images that are unexpected in subject as well as scale.

right: showing an ordinary image in an extraordinary technique or rendering.

below: turning an image at an unexpected angle — like the USA map. (The skeleton just looks a bit more dead!)

15

The principle: CONTRAST WORKS (as long as it is obvious enough — deliberately, strongly done).

The practice: contrast of size.
Left: something big in a small space.
Below: something small in a big space.

OK: Not likely to be putting big feet in a box? How about applying the principle to plain typography?

WAR DECLARED

Bigness in type (or anything else) is the most widely accepted symbol for importance)

Smallness in a big space is even more effective ----

The principle holds true for any other sort of contrast — style, language, material, color etc etc

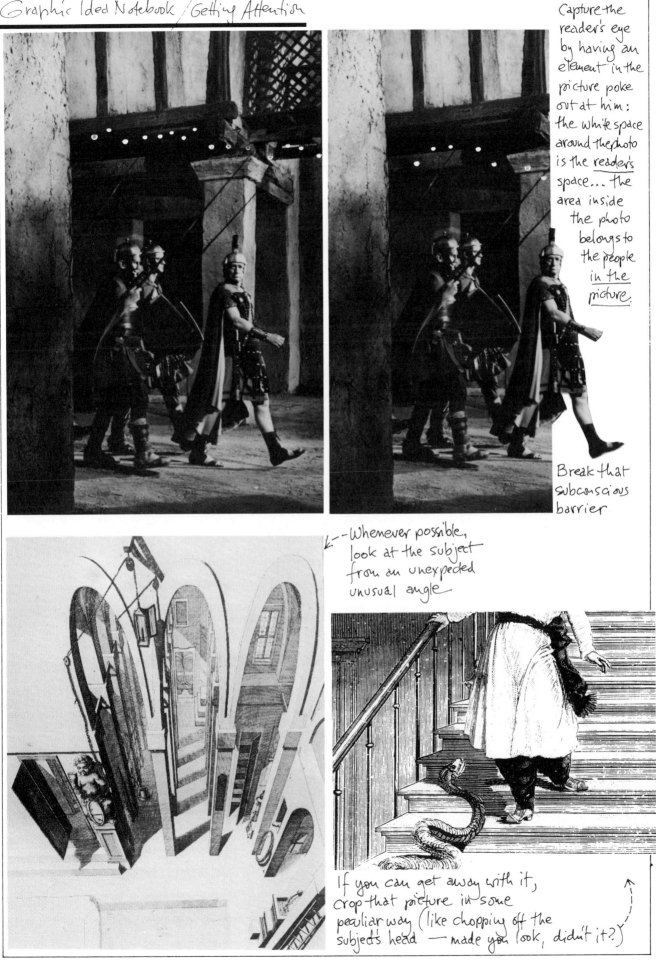

Capture the reader's eye by having an element in the picture poke out at him: the white space around the photo is the reader's space... the area inside the photo belongs to the people in the picture.

Break that subconscious barrier

←--Whenever possible, look at the subject from an unexpected unusual angle

If you can get away with it, crop that picture in some peculiar way (like chopping off the subject's head — made you look, didn't it?)

17

Here's a singularly UNLIKELY subject for glamour — yet by cutting and pasting prints of the three exposures → a startling panorama can be manufactured...

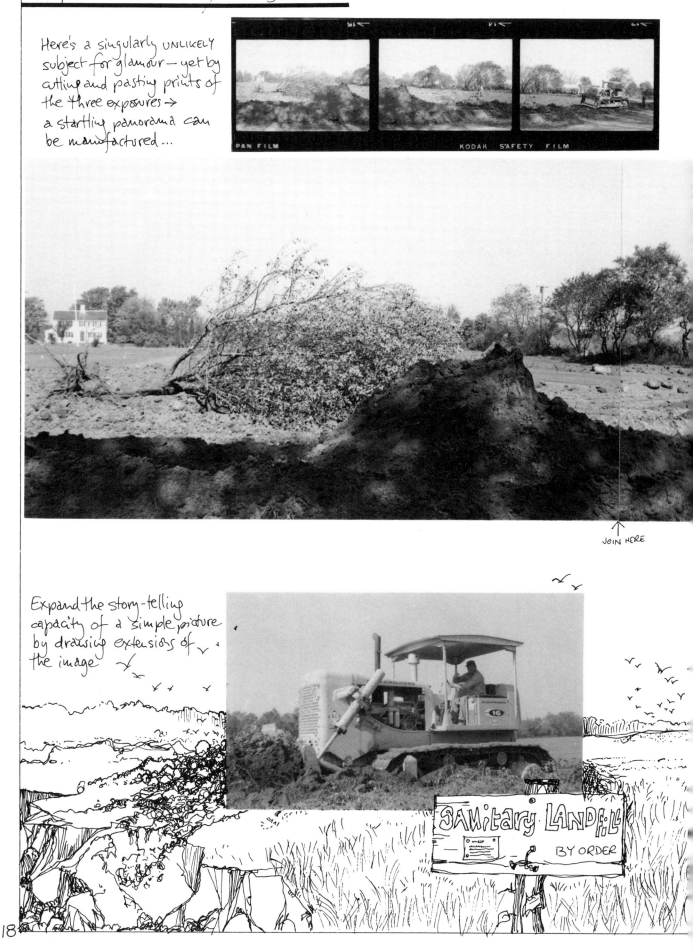

JOIN HERE

Expand the story-telling capacity of a simple picture by drawing extensions of the image

SANITARY LANDFILL BY ORDER

18

A panorama is fine to have on a 2-page spread like this one (true, it would be better if it bled at both sides). But how much more impressive it would be, were it a full 3-page gatefold!

Good   Better   Best   Gatefold

↑ JOIN HERE

Clarify (or draw attention to) an important element on the periphery of a photo by turning that part into a drawing. That way, editorial emphasis can be brought onto an area the reader might well have missed.

This example is the logical outcome of the suggestions on the preceding two pages. It combines the photo with line art in a sense-making relationship, by sharing the WHAT (in the picture) and the HOW (in the drawing). By combining the two into a unified image, the functional interplay between the WHAT and the HOW is brought into focus as an integral element of the story. That's something that would be missing from the usual presentation technique which would show the two independently — one as a photo, the other as a drawing nearby.

(ILLUSTRATION COURTESY OF ARCHITECTURAL RECORD)

Startling effects can be achieved by using words and doing things with them — specially if the words are a bit unusual — — — — — — → and if the type in which they are set is also "different".

Taking a word and running it backwards — or just a piece of it flopped left to right. Or all of it.

Taking a word and cutting the letters apart:

Taking a word and making it into a picture in some way.

Excrescence

RIDICULOUS
SUOLUCIDIR
RIDICULOUS
SUOLUCIDIR

split
shake

AMAZING

Add symbols. It is impossible to show them all. So here are just a few to start the finding process: fists, arrows, bullets, asterisks, stars, squares.

Graphic gimmicks, such as explosions, fireworks, boxes of various kinds...

Whenever the ancient Romans wanted to say
WOWEE! GEE WHIZZ! FANTASTIC! OUTTASIGHT, MAN!
or words to that effect, Latin allowed
them the expletive shown here ———>
(evidently an expression of joy).
Scribes writing it on their manuscripts
saved precious space by putting the
I above the O like this: !. In short
order, the hole in the O got filled in
with ink — and soon it shrunk to a
mere dot of its old self. Hence the : !
(No Kidding — IO !)

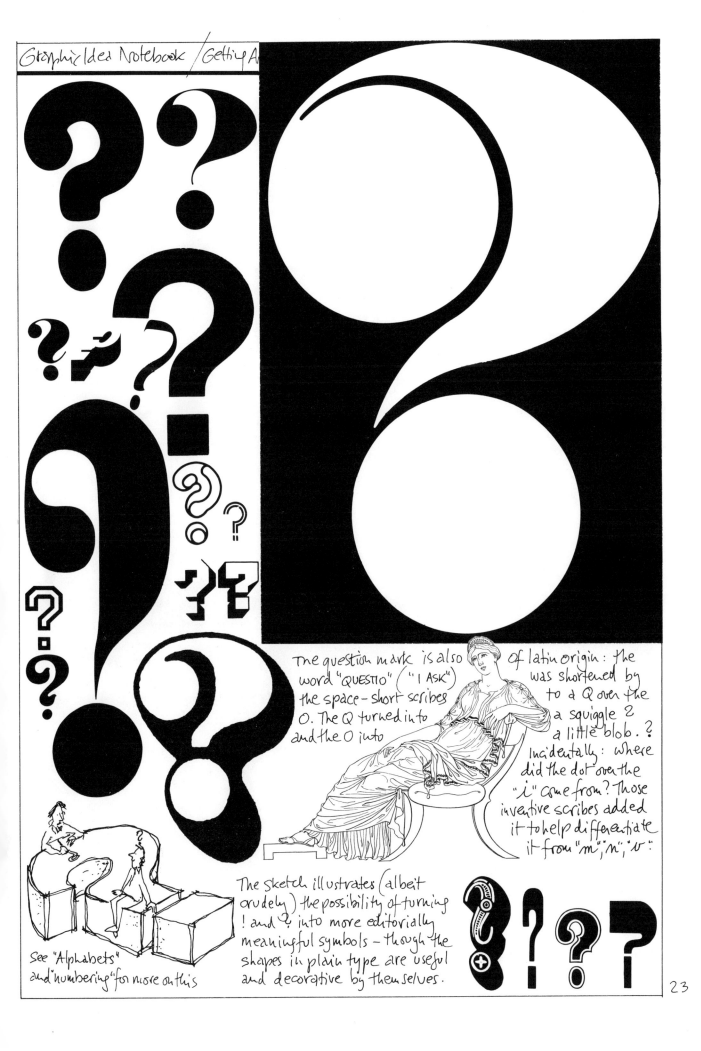

The question mark is also of latin origin: the word "QUESTIO" ("I ASK") was shortened by the space-short scribes to a Q over the O. The Q turned into a squiggle & and the O into a little blob. ?

Incidentally: where did the dot over the "i" come from? Those inventive scribes added it to help differentiate it from "m", "n", "v".

The sketch illustrates (albeit crudely) the possibility of turning ! and ? into more editorially meaningful symbols — though the shapes in plain type are useful and decorative by themselves.

See "Alphabets" and "numbering" for more on this

23

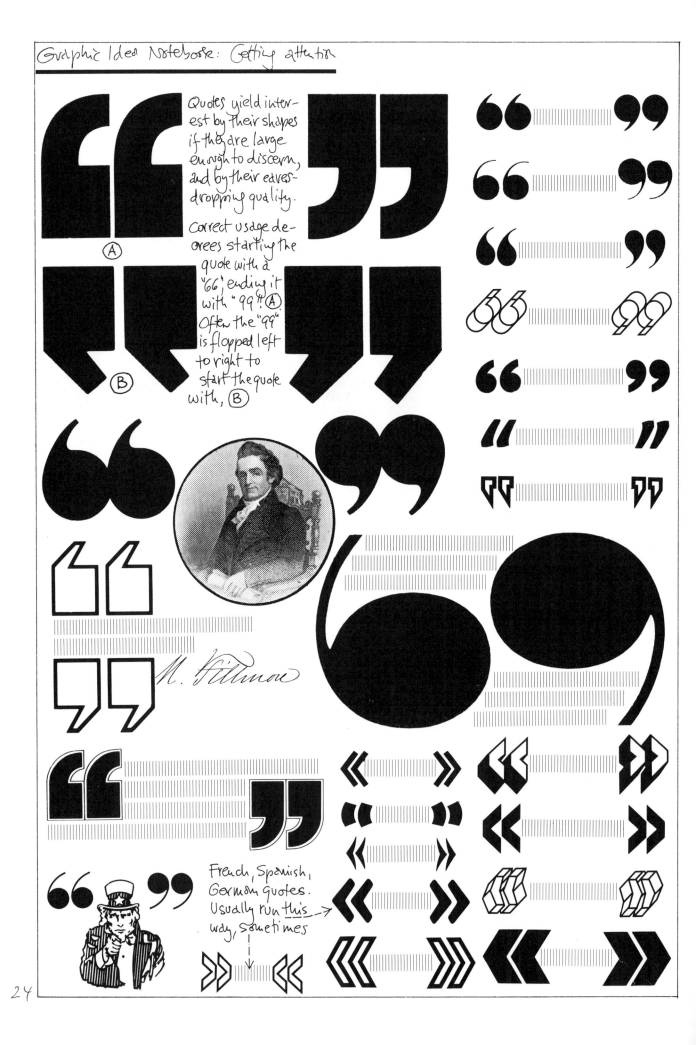

Quotes yield interest by their shapes if they are large enough to discern, and by their eavesdropping quality.

Correct usage decrees starting the quote with a "66," ending it with "99." (A) Often the "99" is flopped left to right to start the quote with. (B)

M. Fillmore

French, Spanish, German quotes. Usually run this way, sometimes

Eleven different ways to handle balloons — just to show a glimpse of the variety of expression that can be achieved:

E ille pellit sensar luptae epicur semperu in indutial genelation. What gitur conve bestis, uae putat esse specula naturae, tat peccage eronylar ian doler, non solud indepra at non sint, lat peccage eronylar ian doler, non solud indepra at non sint, lat peccage eronylar tian doler, non solud at ille pellit sensar luptae epicur semperho in indutial genelation. What gitur conven bestis, uae putat esse specula naturae.

Anno Domini

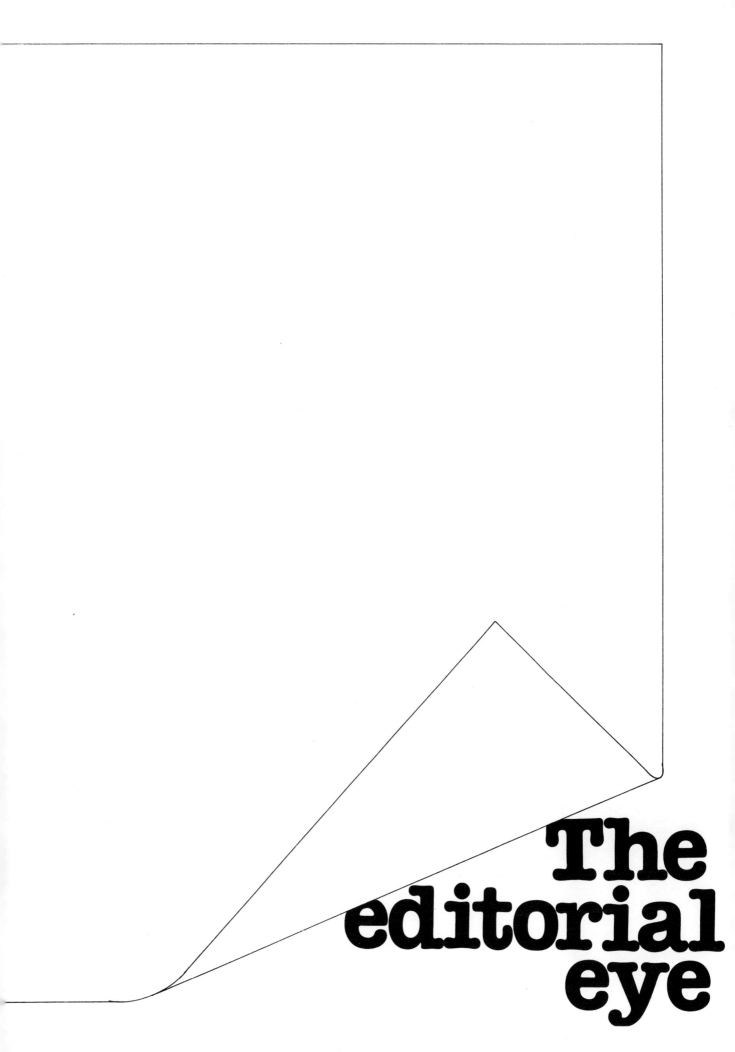

The
editorial
eye

The editorial

The primary criterion for putting anything in a magazine is its *communication value:* What does it tell the reader? The editor must not be bullied into running anything that does not help the story along—least of all by photos. Yet photos are what most often bully the editor because they seem so final, so complete, so immutable, so sacrosanct. Nonsense!

The editor's job is not to win friends (i.e., photographers), but to influence people (i.e., readers). That's why photos must be seen as raw material to be manipulated to the editor's purpose by the skills of the art director, so their latent story-enhancing capacities can be exposed. The story is what matters. Pictures don't—certainly not 99 percent of what gets pub-

lished. They are not art; they are what the camera recorded when it was pointed at something and the shutter was tripped. *Fine* photography does tell a story of its own, and that kind of material is indeed sacrosanct. But for the rest? For that 99 percent you must have the guts to do what follows:

The negative version of an image implies something strange... ghostly... threatening... unpleasant. That might well be more to the point than the straightforward (positive) version of the same image, which would just show what something looks like — albeit more clearly (and its unpleasantness would have to be brought out in words).

←—Flopping the image: illusion of a mirror... duplication... opposition... indecision. Upside-down and under the original it implies a puddle!

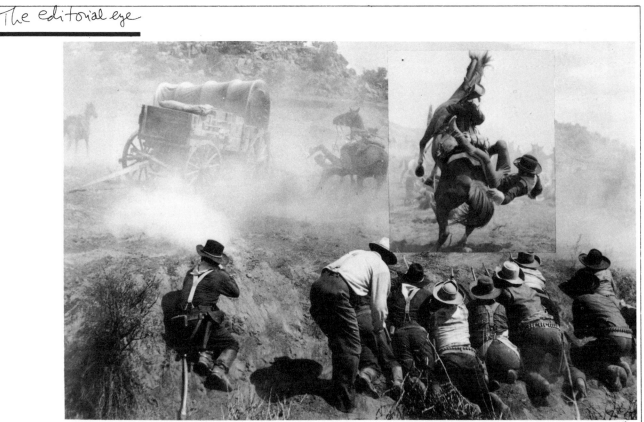

Inserting one image inside another can be like 1+1=3 if the subjects work in concert in meaning as well as in arrangement. Just imagine the impact of a color-picture as the focal point inside the black & white!

Overlapping implies interrelationships. It can only work graphically if a dark area is placed next to a light one. Failing that, use outlines.

VIGNETTES

The hard-edged, rectangular halftone is so standard as to be thought of as virtually the only way of reproducing a photo. But a soft, dissolving outline may well be more suited to a dreamlike, fugitive subject... reinforcing its editorial point.

Second potential advantage: a non-geometric shape adds variety and freshness to the issue as a whole. It lets in some air.

The evanescent edge is made by careful retouching with an airbrush — a tricky art best commissioned from professionals.

Taking vignetting a step further by combining it with normal hard-edge in the same halftone. To draw attention to the point, the ectoplasmic exudation above is larger than the crisp part at right. Better proportion: making the NORMAL part of the picture dominant by size, and the appendix puffing out of it smaller as —→. This was a popular technique in the late 1800s, produced as wood- or steel-engraving rather than photos. But the principle is the same.

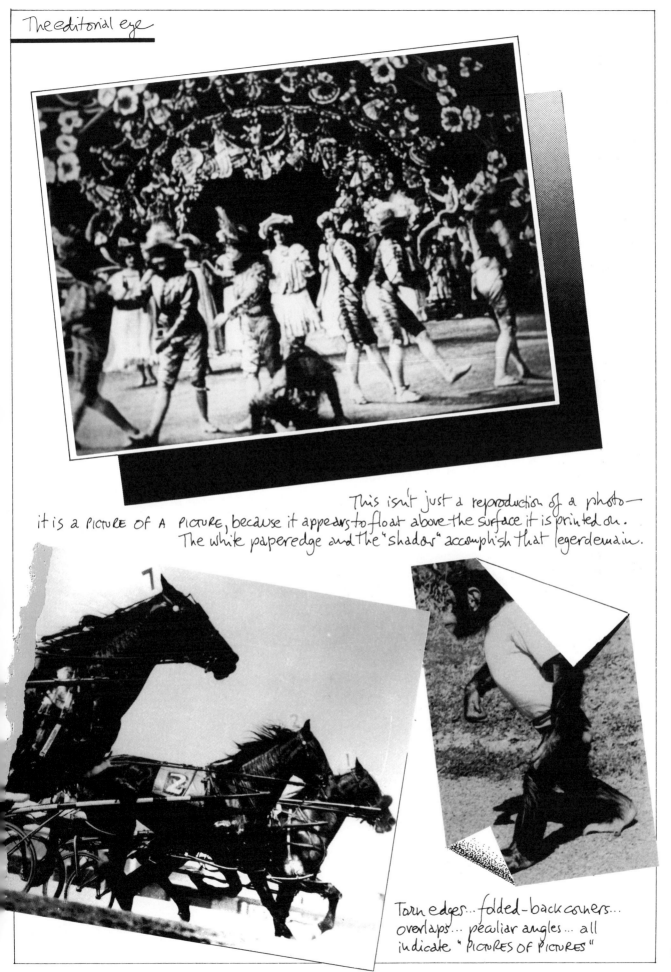

This isn't just a reproduction of a photo— it is a PICTURE OF A PICTURE, because it appears to float above the surface it is printed on. The white paper edge and the "shadow" accomplish that legerdemain.

Torn edges... folded-back corners... overlaps... peculiar angles... all indicate "PICTURES OF PICTURES"

Treat the photo as if it were a view seen through an open window. Add the surrounding walls to create this illusion by screened artwork. (Drawing in the actual windowframe might be logical but it isn't essential except in special situations).

The top should be darkest, the "sill" the lightest in tone. This is a useful trick for combining several interrelated views — but it won't work unless the horizons in all the pictures are carefully aligned.

Express an editorial opinion by "shattering" the glass of the image (i.e. drop-out a line drawing of the broken pieces from the halftone).

Combine two halves of images related in SHAPE as well as in MEANING (e.g. before-and-after, pro-and-con etc)

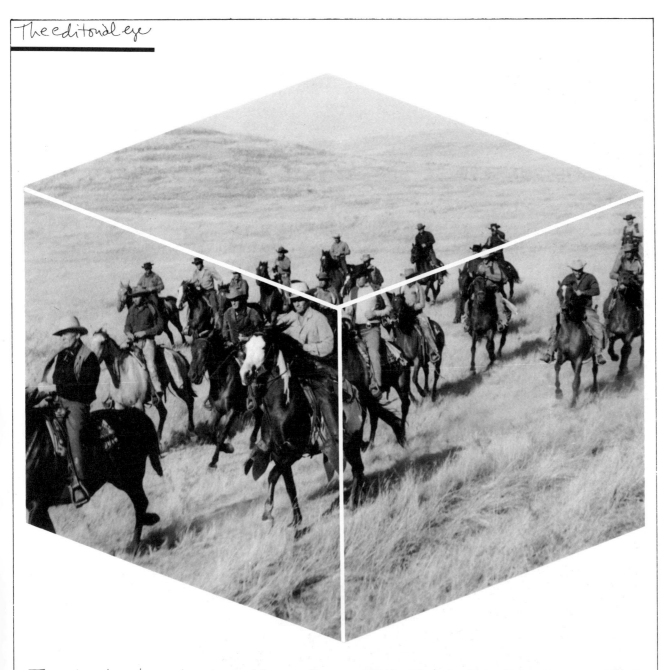

Trim the photo to conform to the shape of a geometrical solid, such as a cube or a cylinder etc. Drop out from the halftone (or surprint, of course) the lines that define the forward edges of the shape ... creating an illusion of dimension that can transform an ordinary photo into an extraordinary impression.

Surround a severely-cropped detail with an elaborate (but "flat" or two-dimensional) frame. Result: the creation of an apparent foreground plane that has a hole in it — ie. the illusion of looking through a keyhole →

Don't just illustrate a scene with a picture, but increase its journalistic impact by physically manipulating it: e.g. emphasizing Activity here by cutting it into staggered strips.

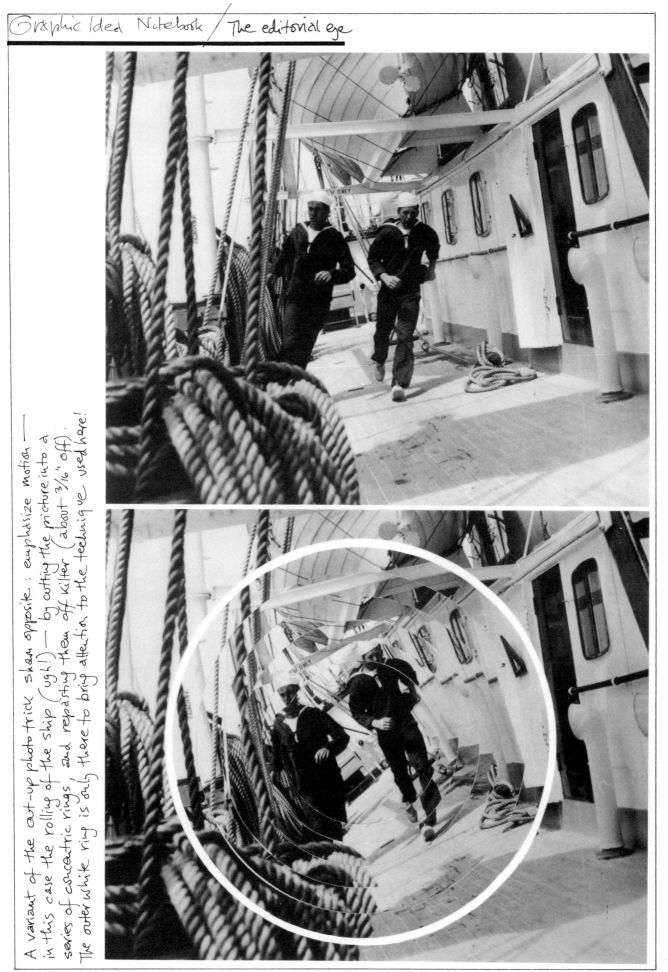

A variant of the cut-up photo-trick shewn opposite : emphasize motion — in this case the rolling of the ship (ugh!) — by cutting the picture into a series of concentric rings, and repasting them off kilter (about 3/16" off). The outer white ring is only there to bring attention to the technique used here!

to point up a part of a picture, where the context in which it is seen must remain, but could be made less important:

1. Pale down the surrounding background (or darken it, if that might be better) by:

• Retouching the photo by spraying on paint — best left to professionals, or...

• Manipulating it by mechanical methods:

The engraver can do it, but needs clear instructions. A simple geometric shape can be shown as a "KEYLINE" overlay. A complex silhouette requires a "MASK" cut from specially-made material. (EASY!)

2. Change the texture of the surroundings by photo-mechanical tricks: The concentric line screen is just one of many options:

The editorial eye

Turning the picture sideways automatically gets attention.

ouch!

On an overlay over the original photo draw, stick on, rub-off, transfer the symbol that will pull the viewer's attention to the crucial element. That symbol is then stripped-in (black) or dropped out (white) by the printer. Common sense will dictate whether to strip-in or drop-out.

Eavesdropping always attracts attention. Listening-in on conversations within the pictures can be shown several ways: by simply placing the words at an angle so they appear to be coming out of a particular personage... by putting them in a call-out area... by placing them in a cartoon-bladder inside or outside the picture... by showing "thoughts" as a picture.

Outline letters can appear TRANSPARENT: an easy illusion to create by surprinting over a simple background (TOP) or dropping out from a dark one (BELOW). But over a mottled one (CENTER) the insides of the letters need to be lightened (or darkened) — here "ghosted" to 60% — by the printer.

THE NAME OF THIS TYPEFACE IS — YOU GUESSED IT — EGYPTIAN OUTLINE! TUT TUT

Words and pictures working together:

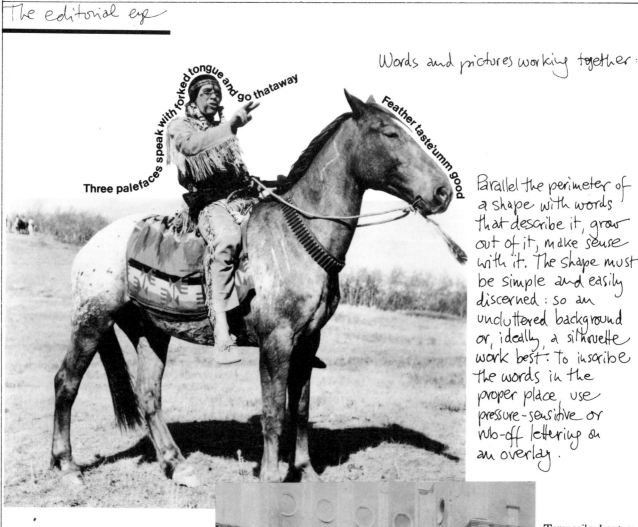

Three palefaces speak with forked tongue and go thataway

Feather taste umm good

Parallel the perimeter of a shape with words that describe it, grow out of it, make sense with it. The shape must be simple and easily discerned: so an uncluttered background or, ideally, a silhouette work best. To inscribe the words in the proper place, use pressure-sensitive or rub-off lettering on an overlay.

To describe the contents of an illustration that shows several separate elements, break the caption into the requisite components and place them around the picture. Lines drawn between the caption and its image may be useful. (Don't try to understand the words here: they are just nonsense—latin "greeking" or "dummy type".)

Temporibud autem delectus ut aut ante cum memorite neque pecun mod and dedocendesse ipsinuria detriment et carum esse iucund quod cuis.

Et tamen in busdam ut coercend magist possit duo conetud praesert cum omning

Lorem ipsum dolor quis nostrud exer consequat, vel illum exceptur sint occaecat

Concupis plusque in vel plurify afferat. Nam dilig sed mult etiam mag tuent tamet eum locum

Euae de virtutib sempitern aut diuter movente propter luptas erit praeder

Temporibud autem quinusd delectus ut aut prefer ante cum memorite tum etia neque pecun modut

I lena sit, ratiodipsa sic amicitian non modo fuerte. Null modo sine oluptation.

Lorem ipsum dolor sit quis nostrud exercitatio consequat, vel illum exceptur sint occaecat

Nam ria detriment est quam et carum esse iucund est quod cuis. Guae ad amicos seque facil, ut mihi detur expedium.

It might be logical to chop up the picture to follow the segmented caption – or even superimpose the captions onto the image to gain impact and fast communication.

Lorem ipsum dolor sit amet, quis nostrud exercitation ullam consequat, vel illum dolore

Temporibud autem delectus ut aut prefer ante cum memorite tum neque pecun modut est

Euae de virtutib dictal sempitern aut diuterning

Combining words and pictures:

The ordinary way to do it is, of course, to "surprint" words in black over the halftone, or to "drop out" words in white from the halftone. (Assuming that black ink is used on white paper; the principle is the same in different hues... This statement ought to be so self-evident that it is unnecessary, but, alas, experience teaches otherwise).

Here are variations — all easy in concept but fairly difficult to achieve, since much "masking", "dropping-out" and preparation is necessary.

The word is part of the picture... the word is in fact "dropped out" from the neighboring color area and the color is allowed to overlap the halftone.

The lower edge of the letters invades the halftone. A sliver of white space is inserted to separate them and increase legibility.

SHADOW

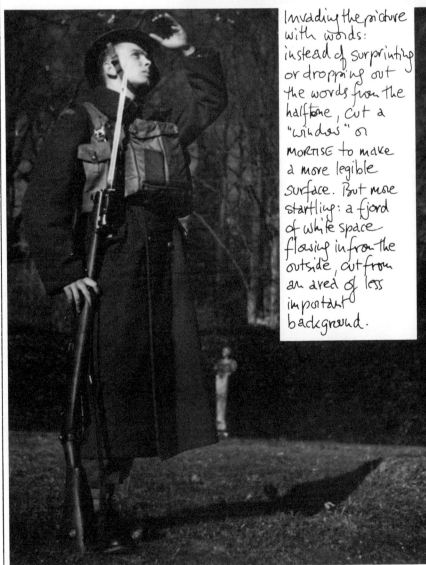

Invading the picture with words: instead of surprinting or dropping out the words from the halftone, cut a "window" or MORTISE to make a more legible surface. But more startling: a fjord of white space flowing in from the outside, cut from an area of less important background.

The picture overlaps into the word. The letters meld into the image, and they are defined by their "shadowed" edges.

Opposite technique to the one above: the letters are simple, but the "shadow" they cast is made of picture.

K

The word and the image are unified. To make this trick work, the picture must have a strong pattern as well as easily-discerned details in it. And the type should be large, bold and tightly set, to make the holes inside and between them minimal.

The word is an integral part of the picture, as in the "PROBLEM" opposite, (here seen against the surrounding white space.) The intrusion into the white space is aggressive and accounts for the shock-value. As in all such tricks, the word must relate to the picture.

Substitute a picture for a letter in a word: as long as the word/image association is clear in meaning, the technique will work even if the image is NOT reminiscent of the shape of the letter that is missing.

GR**O**WTH

Picture same shape as replaced letter — or image used as stuffing inside the letter.

GR**O**WTH

The word/image association can be literal and naturalistic, or symbolic and abstract.

GR**O**WTH

Add little illustrations to the word: either outside the letters or within the strokes of the letters

W**O**RK

It is livelier if the figures are shown intertwined among the letters than just standing on top.

SETTING TYPE IN THE OUTLINE OF A SHAPE SUCH AS THIS IS RARE AND SOMEWHAT UNLIKELY EVENT IN A DESIGNER'S WORKING LIFE BUT THAT SHOULD NOT PRECLUDE ITS VALIDITY AS A TECHNIQUE IF AND WHEN AN OPPORTUNITY ARISES

MOST OF THE GREAT TYPOGRAPHY in America is composed on the Alpha-Type and on the Mergenthaler VIP photo-typesetting systems. These systems use a small piece of film with a complete alphabet in negative form, called a font, to compose your body copy, letter by letter. The font is the heart of the typesetting system. Leonard Storch Enterprises, Inc. is America's First Film Font Foundry and offers the largest selection of both tra-ditional and contemporary alphabet styles. We are the leader, and have created quality stand-ards in font manufac-turing that others can only try to imitate. Well over 500 of America's Lead-ing typographers have chosen Storch Fonts to compose your copy. They made the best choice pos-sible to serve your needs. When your typographer uses Storch Fonts, you have a better chance of getting the job on time, razor sharp, in perfect alignment and proper fit no matter what tightness you specify. We have fostered the art of typography by giving the typesetter "TOOLS" that work better at prices that enable him to stoc k all the alphabets you need. You can help foster the art of typography an d have the world's best body too. Be sure your typog-rapher uses origi nal Storch Fonts.

Setting words in pictorial shapes: visual puns can be useful (on rare occasions). Assuming the validity of the idea, all you need is space, time and money: SPACE for displaying a big image in (it is hard to establish a clear shape in miniature). TIME & MONEY for tinkering with the text and reset-ting the type to get it to fit just right. This example is from an ad for Storch Enterprises talking about "BODY COPY". (REPRODUCED WITH PERMISSION).

45

Graphic Idea Notebook

Combining and joining

JOINING | COMBINING | AND | ASSEMBLING | SO | THAT **2+2=17**

17? That's the whole point. The usual, expected cliche that describes synergetic action where the whole is greater than the sum of its parts is to say that $1 + 1 = 3$. But in this chapter we're talking about more than 1+1—in fact we're talking of groupings (that means a minimum of three to start with, though four is better). Hence the $2 + 2$ in the left-hand part of our equation. But *17*? Well, the expected 5 is weak. Hardly worth the bother. So why *not* 17? If four little items working together can create something four times greater than expected, we're certainly getting more bang for the buck. So let's shoot for the stars.

Yes, this is a "group" but how weak it is! It has the flabbiness of a handshake like this →

The only virtue of this "group" is that the elements are a bit larger; that makes it harder to get them on the page in a row, so the row is split into two and the result READS better AS A GROUP... but it is probably accidental that it does that. It is still unimaginative, weak, and like →

That's better! The "group" has become a deliberate editorial ploy: an attempt to make something more of the material than just running it as is. The group is the nexus — the focal point. This has GUTS ... STRENGTH...

FORTHRIGHTNESS →

The background (patterned geometrical, color or naturalistic ↑) fuses the elements superimposed on it into a unit. Particularly effective if there is common meaning between them ↘

49

Similarity in background color (whether as degrees of blackness or actual hues) can combine a bunch of independent pictures into an organized entity. It works even if the subjects of the pictures vary widely (as in New Product reports etc)

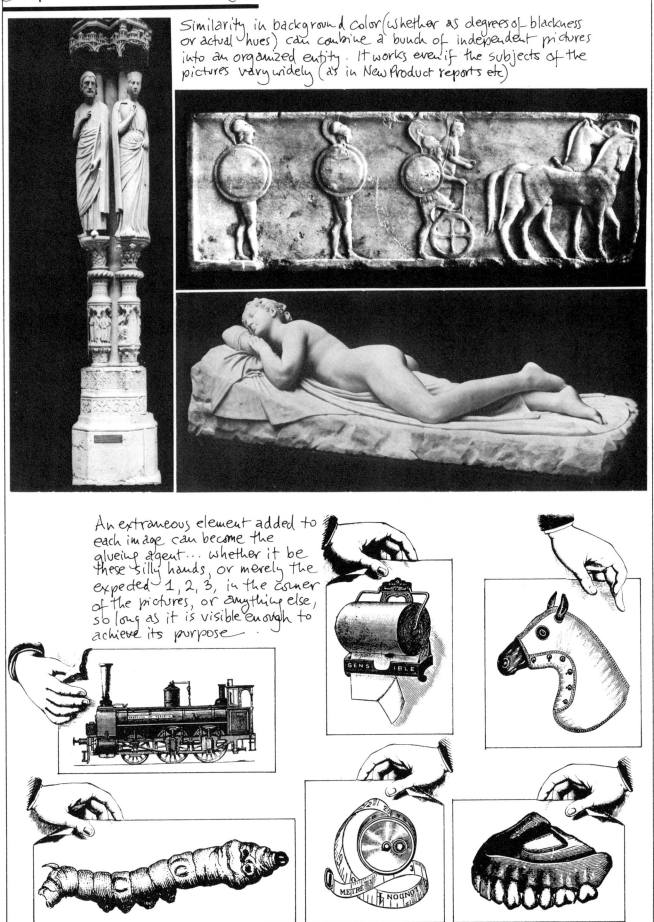

An extraneous element added to each image can become the glueing agent... whether it be these silly hands, or merely the expected 1, 2, 3, in the corner of the pictures, or anything else, so long as it is visible enough to achieve its purpose.

Photo corners to reinforce the illusion

Handwritten captions, of course, more effective if informally placed at an angle. OK, granted — it is corny.*

Treat pictures as articles in themselves — and show them as pictures of pictures (instead of reproductions of their images). As "album", as contact strip, as bits of paper from the photo shop...

* but it works

51

Cropping the photos to form exaggerated shapes: long, thin horizontals or tall, thin verticals... the subjects can be similar (as above) or totally disparate (as at left) yet they ACT as a group because of the cropping.

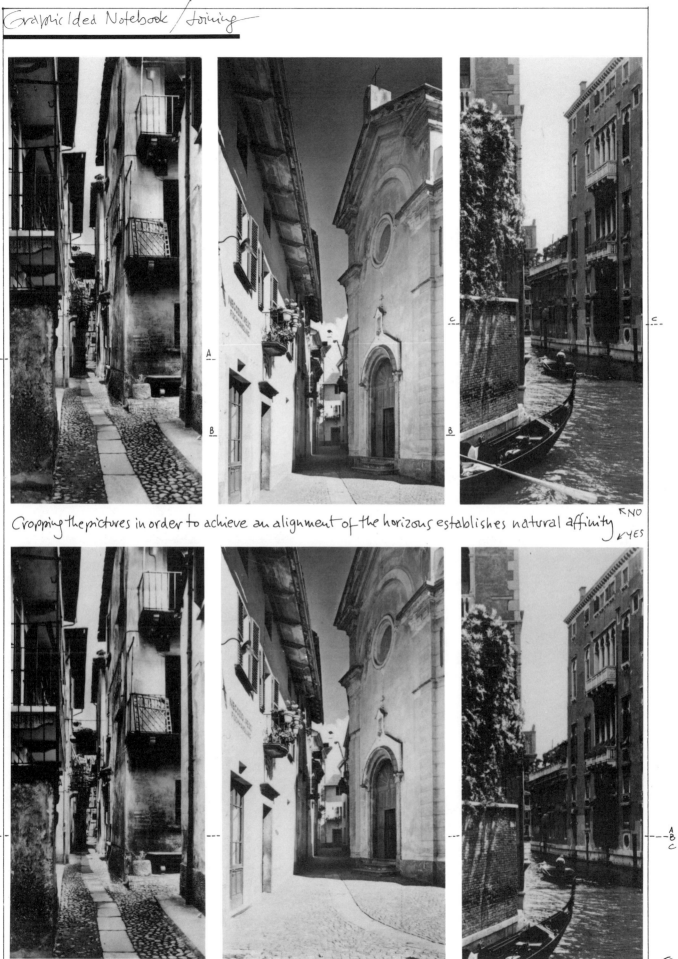

Cropping the pictures in order to achieve an alignment of the horizons establishes natural affinity ↖NO ↙YES

Overlapping not only makes a bigger
arrangement out of a handful of small
units, but it can (though it need not)
be used to imply flow from one image
into the next.

Cropping one side at an
angle automatically
establishes a relationship
among all the photos
thus treated. (MAL treated?)
Placing them in a more
random arrangement on
the page than the elementary
row as here a would make
the trick more powerful.

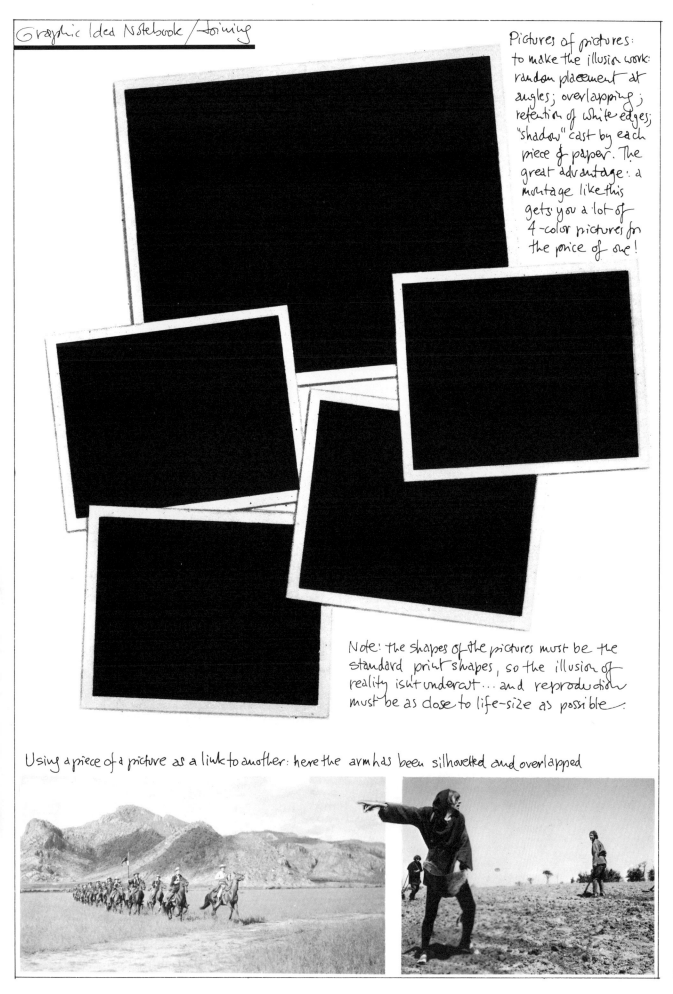

Pictures of pictures: to make the illusion work: random placement at angles; overlapping; retention of white edges; "shadow" cast by each piece of paper. The great advantage: a montage like this gets you a lot of 4-color pictures for the price of one!

Note: the shapes of the pictures must be the standard print shapes, so the illusion of reality isn't undercut... and reproduction must be as close to life-size as possible.

Using a piece of a picture as a link to another: here the arm has been silhouetted and overlapped

55

Tying pictures together
by shared qualities:

The direction in which the subjects are
viewed (looking up or down at them) or
the foreground through which they are seen...

The subject-matter itself:
if it is peculiar enough, it will hold
the pictures together whether they are shown together 2 or in a more random page arrangement

Inlaying the images into a strongly-patterned trellis of like-sized, like-shaped forms or frames.

Subjecting the pictures to an arbitrary shape. This is easy to do, when the amalgamating shape chosen is flat and geometric, ← like this one. But the trick is much more interesting in 3-D. -- However, the doing of it becomes problematic: it is necessary to build the actual box, then to glue on the photos, then to photograph the result. Is it worth it?

57

Linking pictures by implication of meaning, where the subjects in the pictures seem to share some sort of relationship.

Simplest: people who appear to be speaking to each other... more subtle: pointing to each other or throwing elements from one photo to the next.

Corollary to the above:

Taking an image and splitting it in order to broaden its effectiveness. The scene must be obviously recognizable in both the segments, in order to bridge the gap between them.

File Tab (*horizontal*)

Create a consciousness of the material (the paper) being used. Then, whatever is printed on it becomes, by implication, a PART OF something else and thus joined to all the other parts.

Here: file tabs — simplest artwork to produce. At right, a page that → appears to be "floating" (the "shadow" cut from pressure-sensitive material). Below: a sheaf of papers held together by the best possible joining-symbol ↓

Oops!
67

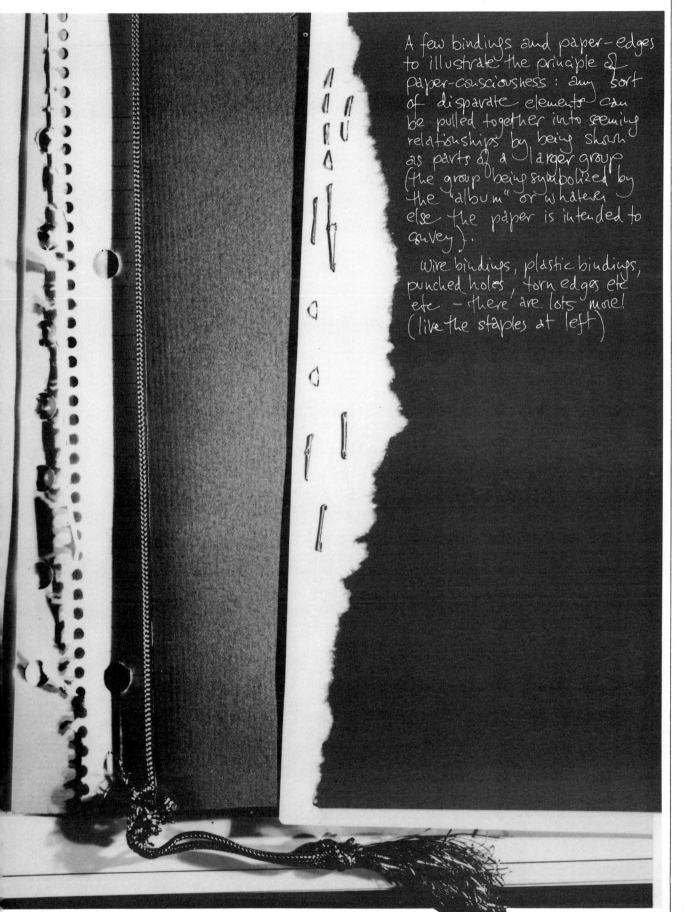

A few bindings and paper-edges to illustrate the principle of paper-consciousness: any sort of disparate elements can be pulled together into seeming relationships by being shown as parts of a larger group (the group being symbolized by the "album" or whatever else the paper is intended to convey).

Wire bindings, plastic bindings, punched holes, torn edges etc etc — there are lots more! (like the staples at left)

(Tying and Fastening)

Using external tools (gimmicks) to tie things together; here's a bunch of obvious ones. Every trade and profession or interest has its own specialized symbols that can be used, added to the general ones shown here. What makes the idea work as a symbol and not a cliché is the graphic handling: it must be right — whatever that may mean — and "interesting". The examples are individually annotated for technique.

Line drawing (pen-and-ink)

Solarization (a photo-mechanical modification of a photo negative)

Photogram or "photo-shadow" (silhouette of an object placed on photographic paper

Tone-line (photo-mechanical process that makes a high contrast version of a photograph)

Ribbon (drawing)

Net

Thread

Barbed wire — ouch!

knot

Belt

Buttons

Garter

Rings
Handcuffs!

Suspenders

Staples

More objects usable as
links; most of them
are old "engravings" from
catalogs — steel engravings,
woodcuts etc. They have
a vitality and colorfulness
hard to duplicate —
even if they aren't quite
as believable as
photographs are.

An old engraving of a screw — and a tone-line version

The rope is a
line drawing

The plastic binder
is a "direct positive"
high-contrast photo.

— and don't forget rubber bands!

A congeries of connectors,
many of them specifically designed
to join paper...
In this photo-montage
the pieces appear to be
"floating" because they
were placed on a thick
sheet of glass and then
lit from two sides. The
shadows appear to be
further away from where
they would normally be.
because of that glass.

Here are most of the same artifacts in the photo on the preceding two pages but reproduced here in a more useable technique: the photogram (or "shadowgram"). They are shown life-size here — that's why they appear so overwhelming: in the miniaturized context of a magazine page they ought to be photographically reduced a bit in size to make them more comfortable —— unless drama is what's needed, in which case anything goes!

AND: the obvious non-pictorial link. The ampersand is the only character aside from "a" that represents a whole word (not just a sound). It comes from the latin ET (ie. "and"). Scribes scribbled it, type designers embellished it, and the result? The character with the most delight and graphic variety in the alphabet. As such, a resource of visual richness — if used flamboyantly!

Alternate symbols: the mathematical PLUS and the word AND (available as a unit in old type books — very Victorian).

Just a random sampling to show the visual
riches in such a simple thing as parentheses.
Each typeface has its own — enjoy!

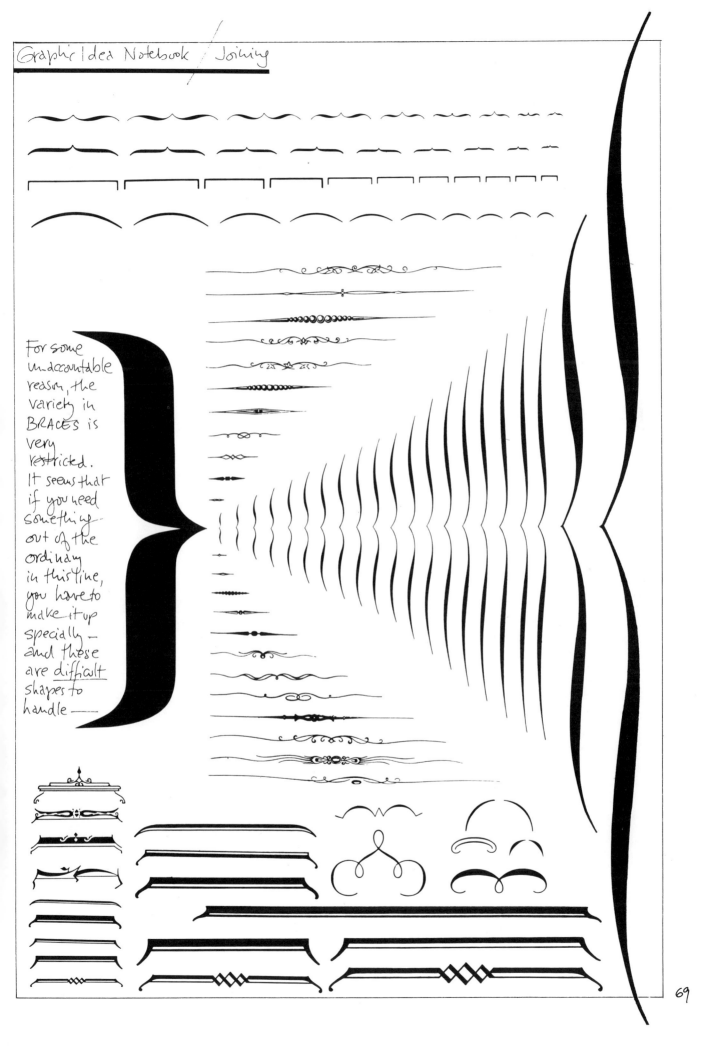

For some unaccountable reason, the variety in BRACES is very restricted. It seems that if you need something out of the ordinary in this line, you have to make it up specially — and these are difficult shapes to handle ——

Graphic Idea Notebook

Graphic Idea Notebook

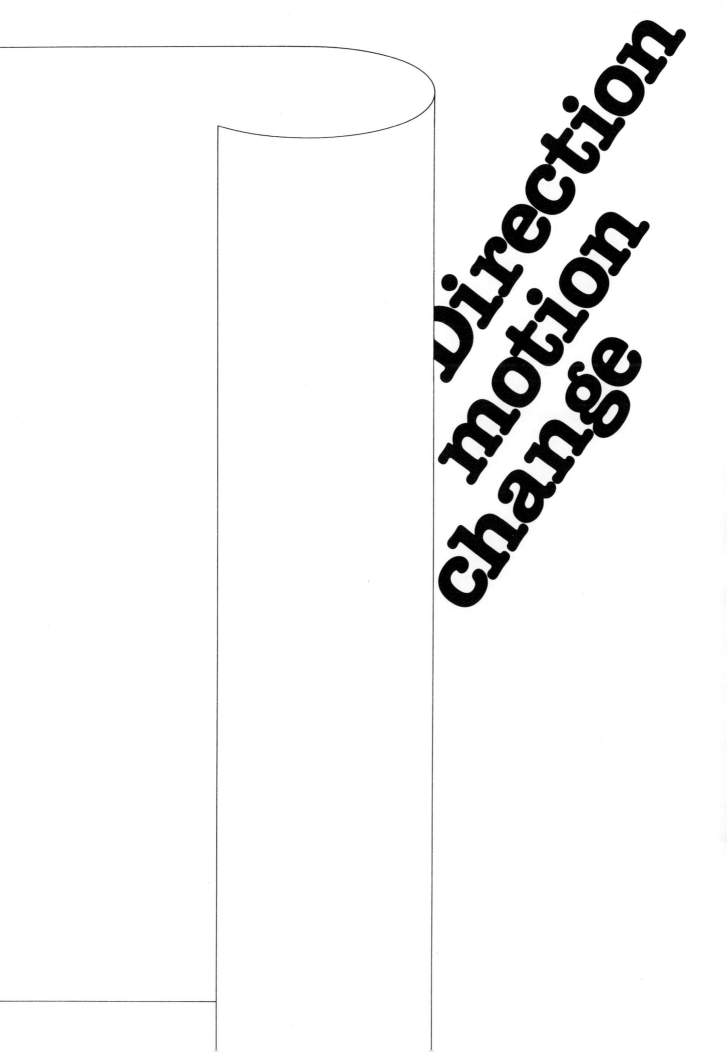

Direction
motion
change

Directionmotionchange

Arrows and "fists" point to something and we know what is expected of us: We follow them out of curiosity—or fear of the law. They are our accepted directional symbols/signs.

But our accumulated experience makes us respond to lines of force or lines of direction that we only *feel*—without actually *seeing* them. We instinctively follow the lines of action depicted in an illustration. We empathize with the chap in a photo and follow his gaze. (Who hasn't looked up at the sky, copying someone else who is doing it—out of magnetic curiosity? The same works with people in pictures, if those pictures are strong.) We understand that a decrease in size implies receding into distance; that's what linear perspective is all about. We understand, equally, that the further away an object is, the more the mists that separate it from the viewer interpose themselves between, thus making that object paler (as well as smaller).

And it is just a short step from showing *direction* to showing *motion*. . .and from motion to *change*. The following pages are devoted to them. Have fun.

Fists can vary from the most severely stylized to the most naturalistic.

Yet the force of direction set up by them is inescapable

Perhaps this is going a bit too far?

The majority of printers' fists are masculine. (Why?)

A strongly directional alphabet — for use only with great restraint!

A B C D
E F G H I J K L
M N O P Q R S T
U V W X Y Z

RETURNED TO SENDER

73

Footnote: Mouse   rabbit   squirrel   raccoon

The only successful swords–into–plowshares transformation in human history: weapon into harmless directional symbol, universally understood. All these variations available as rub-off, cut-out, paste-on art in various sizes from various manufacturers.

THIS IS WHAT YOU NEED FOR REAL DURABILITY

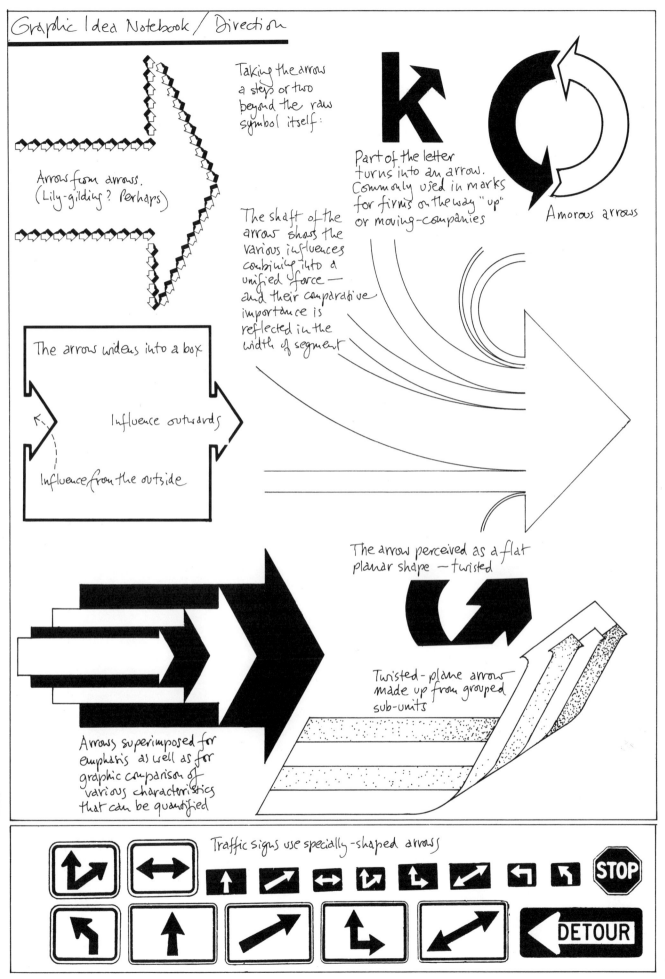

Arrows from arrows.
(Lily-gilding? Perhaps)

Taking the arrow a step or two beyond the raw symbol itself:

Part of the letter turns into an arrow. Commonly used in marks for firms on the way "up" or moving-companies

Amorous arrows

The shaft of the arrow shows the various influences combining into a unified force — and their comparative importance is reflected in the width of segment

The arrows widens into a box

Influence outwards

Influence from the outside

The arrow perceived as a flat planar shape — twisted

Twisted-plane arrow made up from grouped sub-units

Arrows superimposed for emphasis as well as for graphic comparison of various characteristics that can be quantified

Traffic signs use specially-shaped arrows

STOP

DETOUR

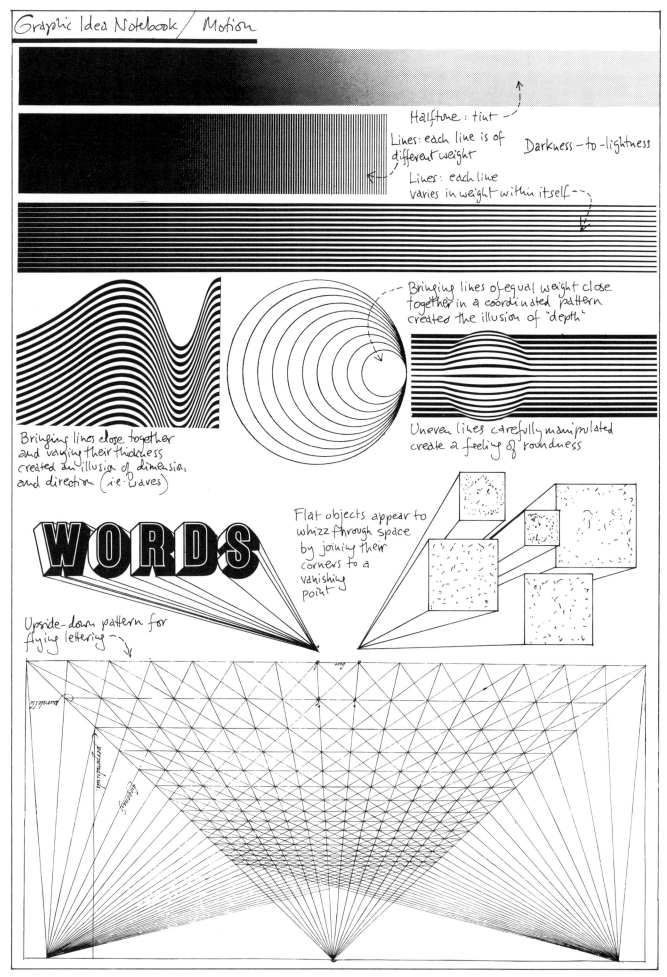

Halftone: tint

Lines: each line is of different weight

Darkness-to-lightness

Lines: each line varies in weight within itself

Bringing lines of equal weight close together in a coordinated pattern created the illusion of "depth"

Bringing lines close together and varying their thickness created an illusion of dimension and direction (i.e. waves)

Uneven lines carefully manipulated create a feeling of roundness

WORDS

Flat objects appear to whizz through space by joining their corners to a vanishing point

Upside-down pattern for flying lettering

parallel

perpendicular

diagonal

76

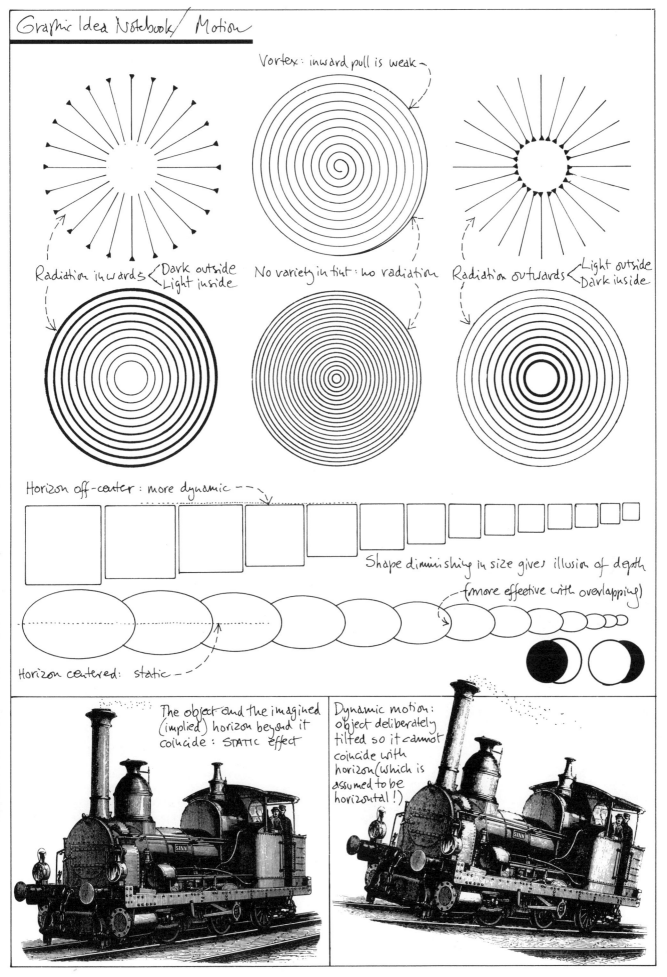

Vortex: inward pull is weak →

Radiation inwards ⟨ Dark outside
Light inside

No variety in tint : no radiation

Radiation outwards ⟨ Light outside
Dark inside

Horizon off-center : more dynamic - - →

Shape diminishing in size gives illusion of depth
(more effective with overlapping)

Horizon centered : static - -

The object and the imagined
(implied) horizon beyond it
coincide : STATIC effect

Dynamic motion:
object deliberately
tilted so it cannot
coincide with
horizon (which is
assumed to be
horizontal !)

... continued from FOLIO's December '77 issue

Graphic Idea Notebook / Motion

Showing actual motion of the action — obviously

Motion completely unseen but implied: the movement past this chap must have been extremely fast!

Competition between subjects in the illustration clearly shows the strain required to achieve the speed needed for victory: immediate viewer-involvement.

Series of objects expected to be moving moves (except when there are traffic jams)

Disappearing: the same subject shown in increasing degrees of "ghosting" (expressed in % of normal).

Stop-motion (time lapse) photography repeated to yield a longer sequence

Note various effects achieved by bumping into edge, breaking through it, and, below, stopping short

® TM, COURTESY OF U.S. TROTTING ASSOCIATION

One image split into slivers, each of which shows a slightly changed portion of the original

Butting the halftones helps smooth transition and emphasizes the changes.

When there are no pictorial images available, plain words suitably played with can be made into striking (or amusing) substitutes. To denote POSITION, the whole trick is to establish simple DATUMS and then work the word around them.
(Rub-off or pressure-sensitive lettering is easy to use).

VERTICAL DATUM

HORIZONTAL DATUM

PIVOTAL DATUM

OVER

UNDER

BELOW

FLOATING

SINKING

SUNK

REFLE NOITC

THROUGH

BOUNCING

UPHILL

The left-to-right flow is fundamental reason why this works

SURROUNDING

INSIDE

OUTSIDE

PIVOTING

VANISHING AND...   ...REAPPEARING

SENTENCES THAT FOLLOW THE DOWNWARD TREND OF THE WAVERING STOCKMARKET

Particularly useful to dress up dull headlines with ↗

To show motion or action, add the direction-lines in the appropriate direction. But beware of curved lines: they can be misinterpreted as fungoid whiskers growing out of the word instead of lines of force!

SURGE

"Birds" are always a suggestion of space and depth

SPRINT

POLLUTE

PLUMMET

EXHAUST

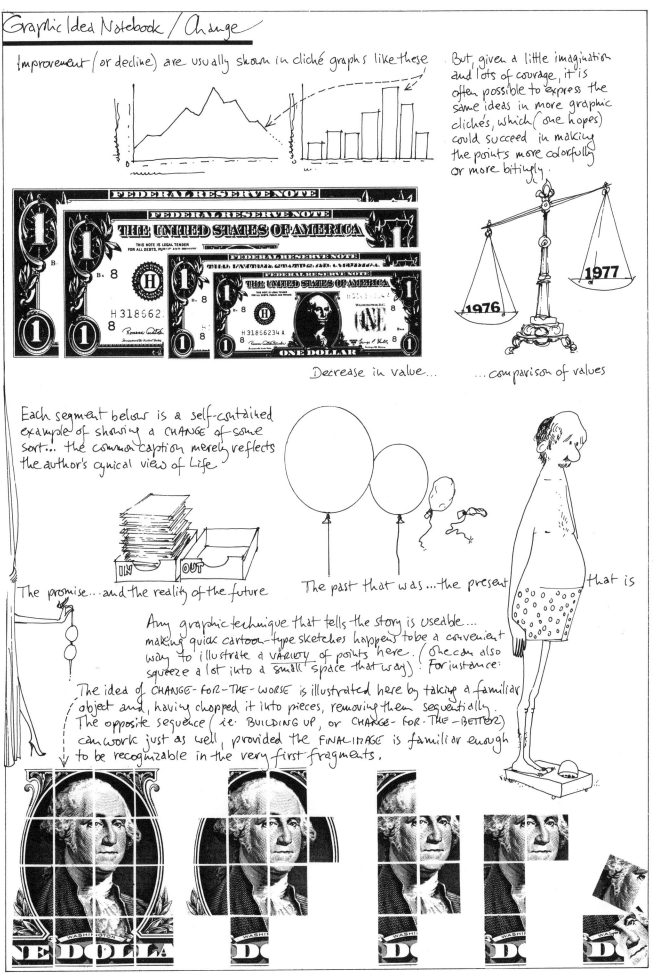

Improvement (or decline) are usually shown in cliché graphs like these

But, given a little imagination and lots of courage, it is often possible to express the same ideas in more graphic cliché's, which (one hopes) could succeed in making the points more colorfully or more bitingly.

1976   1977

Decrease in value...   ...comparison of values

Each segment below is a self-contained example of showing a CHANGE of some sort... the common caption merely reflects the author's cynical view of life

The promise...and the reality of the future   The past that was...the present that is

Any graphic technique that tells the story is useable... making quick cartoon-type sketches happens to be a convenient way to illustrate a VARIETY of points here. (One can also squeeze a lot into a small space that way). For instance:

The idea of CHANGE-FOR-THE-WORSE is illustrated here by taking a familiar object and, having chopped it into pieces, removing them sequentially. The opposite sequence (ie. BUILDING UP, or CHANGE-FOR-THE-BETTER) can work just as well, provided the FINAL IMAGE is familiar enough to be recognizable in the very first fragments.

Passage of time

Signs of the Zodiac

Chinese calendar

Clock faces: (left to right) arabic numerals, roman numerals, victorian embellishments, seconds, mirror image (to startle with), 24-hour clock

19221923192419251926 1927192819291930193119 32 1933193419351936193719 38193919401941194219 43 1944194519461947194819 49195019511952195319 54 195519561957195819 59 19 601961196219631964 1965 19661967196819691970 19 71197219731974 197 51976

'82 '83 '72
'81   '73
'80   '74
'79   75
'78 '77 '76

The passing of years: in a neat geometric array -----> or borrowing the clock symbol <----

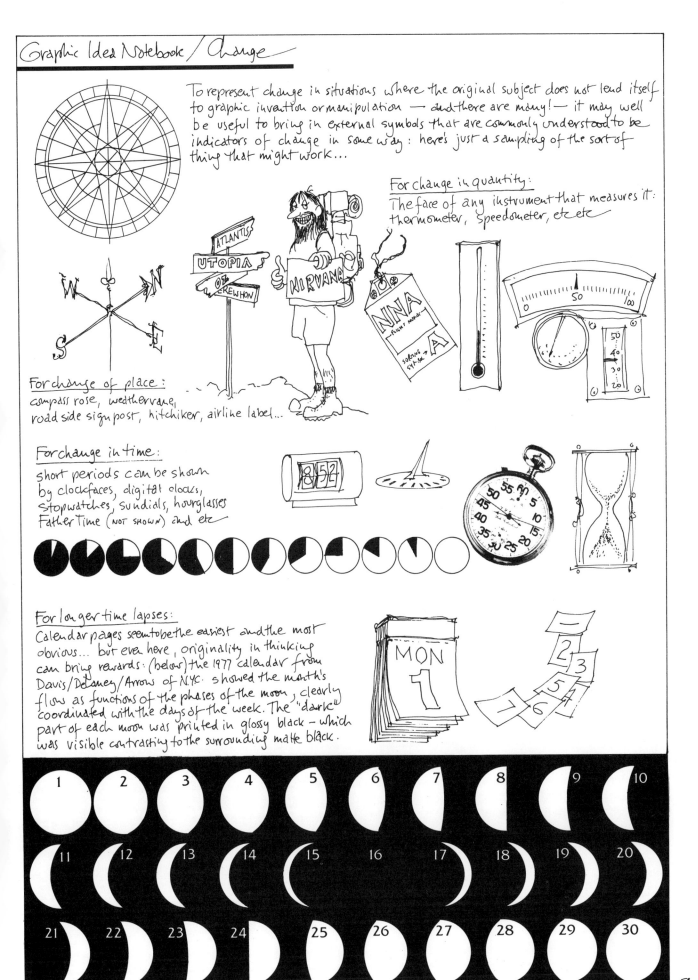

To represent change in situations where the original subject does not lend itself to graphic invention or manipulation — and there are many! — it may well be useful to bring in external symbols that are commonly understood to be indicators of change in some way: here's just a sampling of the sort of thing that might work...

For change in quantity:
The face of any instrument that measures it: thermometer, speedometer, etc etc

For change of place:
compass rose, weathervane, road side signpost, hitchiker, airline label...

For change in time:
short periods can be shown by clockfaces, digital clocks, stopwatches, sundials, hourglasses Father Time (NOT SHOWN) and etc

For longer time lapses:
Calendar pages seem to be the easiest and the most obvious... but even here, originality in thinking can bring rewards: (below) the 1977 calendar from Davis/Delaney/Arrow of N.Y.C. showed the month's flow as functions of the phases of the moon, clearly coordinated with the days of the week. The "dark" part of each moon was printed in glossy black — which was visible contrasting to the surrounding matte black.

Graphic Idea Notebook

Mugshots

MUGSHOTS

Most of them are a bore. So why do we run them? Simply because too often there's nothing else available and all we are stuck with is the picture of the author or the personality being reported on.

But just because that handout portrait of dubious quality is a personal document doesn't necessarily mean that it is God-given and therefore sacrosanct. It doesn't mean that our imagination may not be used or our ingenuity must lie fallow. Sure, sometimes it may be foolhardy to take liberties with those mugshots; yet often a bit of dangerous living adds spice and unexpected freshness to that same old mix.

It is the context in which the mugshot is used, the editorial purpose to which it is put and the personality of the personage that are the criteria on which editors must base their judgment on whether to run the picture as a straight portrait or whether to use it as raw material with inherent graphic malleability.

When should a portrait photo be more than a mugshot? When it can embody a thought or express a point; when it can illustrate a thought; when it can do more than just show the reader what somebody's face looks like.

When should a mugshot be used as a straight portrait? When it happens to be a picture of someone who depends on his or her face for recognition—actors, politicians, the Beautiful People, etc. Taking liberties with their physiognomies might be dangerous to their image or livelihood. But the vast majority of unBeautiful People whose

mugs we run will only object for reason of wounded vanity—a hurt that ought to be easily assuaged by the very fact of their being published at all!

Mugshots

1. Choose a simple one. This ought not to be too difficult since most studio shots come that way—a lump in the foreground, with a background of some nondescript kind. But if the background is distracting or unattractive (or if the mugshot has to be taken from a picture that is a candid and contains other visual matter), then something must be done to improve it. Anything that takes attention away from the subject is suspect. So retouch it by lightening, darkening, fuzzing it up; replacing it with something else . . .

2. Consider silhouetting the background away altogether. It is a simple process, especially if the face is facing the camera for then there is no danger of chopping off the proboscis (and if an ear or two disappears by accident, no great loss in recognition value is incurred).

3. For a group of interrelated mugshots, try to unify the background tones in lightness or darkness or texture. Purpose: To make the group read as a group rather than a bunch of odds-and-ends merely run in close proximity. Nothing pulls images of people together more effectively than a unified background—even if those images are widely spaced on the pages.

4. Wherever there is choice, pick the mugshot that illuminates the subject's character rather than just illustrating physical characteristics. If

the subject can get mad at you for having picked *that* one, you may be sure that you are on the right track.

5. If you are lucky enough to get mugshots that show more than just the head, don't crop away all that potentially interesting and pictorial material just because you are going to run a picture of a person. There is no law that says that a mugshot must chop off the head three fingers'-worth below the necktie knot; show the rest as well, especially the hands. Not only are hands expressive in themselves, but they are usually active in some way. And any activity is better than none.

6. Take that original photo and refuse to reproduce it as a plain halftone; that is the expected, the normal, the uninteresting way.

All that is needed is screens ingenuity, some equipment (most probably available at the printer's right now) and—most of all—the desire, as well as the courage, to have fun.

7. What is "expensive?" The investment that doesn't pay off; the graphic effect that remains unnoticed. So, if you do invest in a trick or two, go whole hog and run it big (or in a highly visible way). The kudos you get for originality will justify that extra first cost.

8. With the printed image ready, whether it be the normal halftone or any of the doctored variations shown here, you can manipulate them on the page in lots of fresh ways—by boxing, overlapping, framing, repeating, shaping . . . what have you.

Graphic Idea Notebook

The expected rectangle   Circle   Rounded corners   Diamond   Oval   ... or something else

Just because a mugshot starts out as a rectangular shape doesn't mean that it must be reproduced that way

The simple factor of unexpected size can give life to an ordinary image. But there is a sensible minimum

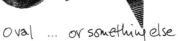

and a logical maximum. ——> At the small size, the face ought to be well-known to start with. At the large size the face ought to belong to someone worthy of seeing so large.

Courageous cropping:

Very tight

Exaggerated vertical

Exaggerated horizontal
(more impressive at larger size than shown here!)

Cropping at an angle changes both direction and mood of subject

87

Graphic Idea Notebook: Mugshots

Silhouette ... with boxes:

Plain

Regular box

Box with peculiar shape

Box with peculiar "color"

Box that determines shape of mugshot within it

Box that is evidently too small to contain its occupant

Box with some appropriate graphic symbolism that helps position the subject in some way

Silhouette ... with backgrounds:

Background with special shape

Background adding 3-D illusion

Background adds color

Background adds texture

16 ANDY

Names

Numbers

Evocative images

Silhouettes combined with other elements in the story

Mugshots presented as "pictures of pictures"
(for best effect, show a group of several, rather than just one)

with photo-corners

stamp

35mm transparency in its sleeve

TV screen

Casting a shadow

89

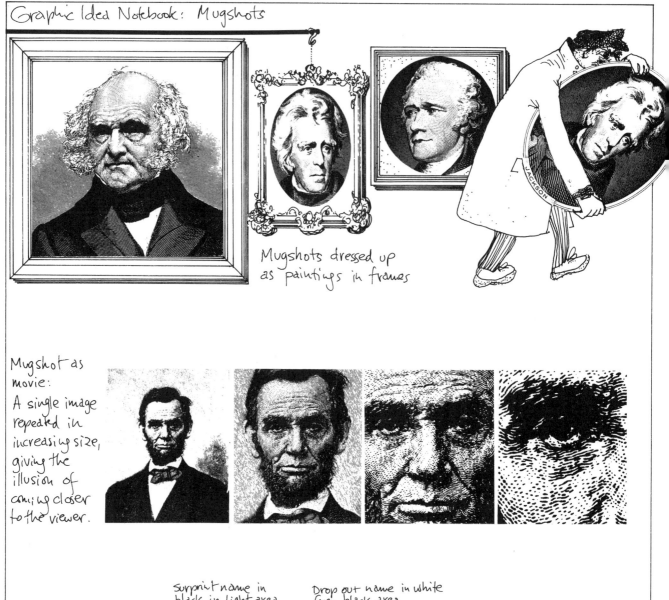

Mugshots dressed up
as paintings in frames

Mugshot as
movie:
A single image
repeated in
increasing size,
giving the
illusion of
coming closer
to the viewer.

THE OBVIOUS PLACE

Surprint name in
black in light area

Drop out name in white
from black area

Name goes here
subtly placed
inside the box

Where does the name go?

Names, affiliations,
pertinent data,
quotes etc can all
enliven the mugshot
presentation — if
they are designed
in from the start.

The name can go here

The name goes here

My name is....

Graphic Idea Notebook: Mugshots

Combining mugshots:

Faces (only) cut out, and overlapped into a unified group

Heads silhouetted; shoulders overlapped

Simple silhouettes superimposed on a unifying background. <u>Above</u>: an abstract pattern. <u>At left</u>: a more symbolic or evocative background (foreground?)

Faces attached to sketched bodies (can serve a serious purpose)

Varying the scale by having some mugs larger than others makes groups that are far livelier

←— For an effectively "unified" group keep all the eyes at the same level

Combining two or more similar units with a contrasting, dominant one —↘

Arbitrary, geometrical grouping made up of units of equal size and shape ——→

Make an overlapping arrangement, where the elements appear to have been placed at random.

A random arrangement is more interesting than a rigid one

Insert a bunch of complex shapes within a larger "container" whose shape is simple to discern. (A square).

←Alternate arrangement— one of hundreds

Conventional wisdom (sensibly) decrees that mugshots face INTO the spread. → or toward each other, if a relationship between the parties is implied ↴

Facing the mugshot outward can pull the reader overleaf by curiosity, following the subject's gaze. But the story had better continue overleaf!

Repetition of mugs on successive pages uses them as a linking device to tie the story together & give it its uniqueness. But this can only work if the shape of each mug and the placement of each is precisely the same as the others.

Placing vertical columns of mugshots between columns of type creates an enlivening rhythm, using even the most pedestrian of raw materials.

A

B

C

Clustering mugshots: assembling groups of people-pictures in deliberately UNEQUAL sizes. This can look amusing and attractive, but such liveliness can be misinterpreted as editorializing since BIG can be thought to mean "IMPORTANT!"

Attaching mug shots to rules: this doubles the effectiveness of the page by doubling the graphic patterns on it: the horizontal pattern (pictorial, photographic) and the vertical pattern (rules, geometric). In version Ⓐ the horizontal emphasis created by the mugshots and the alignment of the text-tops is strong enough to camouflage the irregularity of text lengths... in Ⓑ each vertical shish-kebab of rule-plus-mugshots is identical, but their placement on the page is staggered to yield interesting-looking variety... in Ⓒ the rigidity of the checkerboard pattern in which the mugshots are placed is broken by the rhythmic placement of the rules, as well as arbitrary omissions of a mugshot here or there. Playing with these elements — standard and ordinary raw materials though they be — can lead to original and attractive pages! Pre-requisite: to perceive the mugshots in terms of units in an overall pattern.

Silhouetting and overlapping mugshots (this is where most fun lies) examples: Ⓓ running the frieze at the head of the page, hanging the text down from it. Ⓔ Putting the mugs across the foot of the page and making the most of the ragged gap between them and the text. Ⓕ Creating illusions of scenes of people receding in space (aligned text columns!) etc

D

E

F

FRANK LESLIE

A familiar theme — and 40 variations
on it by Carl Moreus of Norwalk PhotoGraphics.
The old engraving above is made of lines,
each painstakingly engraved by hand. The same
effect of texture is done mechanically in the
camera ↓

Halftone printed as "normally" as possible

The plain halftone (unadorned)

Halftone printed with more contrasts in tones

Halftone silhouetted — with a box

Straight line screen

Screen can go at any angle

Image shown silhouetted as a reminder that
all these screens can be treated as silhouettes

Concentric line screen

Center of screen focuses on important point

Wavy line screen

95

Cut line screen

Linen screen

Steel engraving screen

Steel etch screen

Fine grain screen

Coarse grain screen

Fine mezzotint screen

Coarse mezzotint screen

Burlap screen

Fine wood grain screen

Medium wood grain screen

Coarse wood grain screen

Terry screen

Mesh screen

Image printed through textured glass

High-contrast line plate

more dramatic ~

shows more detail ~

Tone-line conversion

(Negative shown as a reminder that all these screens can be shown as negatives)

Tone-line run as negative

Solid line silhouette

Silhouette negative

Bas-relief

Solarized image

high contrast

Solarized image

normal contrast

Two tints of gray surrounded by a 10% background screen

Posterization

A copy of a copy of a copy done on a copying machine

Xerographic distortion

Xerographic double-image

Xerographic images superimposed

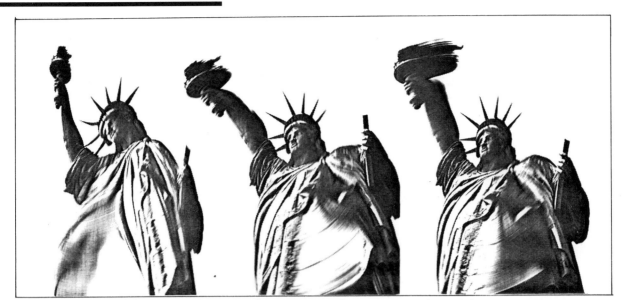

Distortions produced by moving the image during exposure to the xerographic printing process

Distortion of a textured original   Xerographic copy sandwiched to a film-positive duplicate exposed as one

Multiple images   Patterning of double-images as above

99

Watercolor rendering

Brush-and-ink sketch

The subject's personality should be exposed by the talent, insight and skill of the interpreter— be it in photographic or hand-drawn form. The very materials the artist uses to draw with affect the viewer's attitude. Here are 9 examples by Emil Weiss...

Soft crayon rendering

Pen-and-ink drawing *

Gouache * (poster color) rendering

Pencil sketch *

*
Shown at
original size
to demonstrate
character of
draftsmanship

Brush-and-ink
with chalks

Dry brush with
watercolor ~ *

* Dry-brush

Showing mugshots from unexpected angles makes
them much more interesting...
but showing more of the subject than just
the face helps give life to the personality. The
merest indication of a hand implies activity.

Boxes

BOXES

What's in them for you? A lot— as long as they aren't the usual half- or one-point rules assembled by the printer to encase your sidebar in its coffin; that's *dead*. Here are some alternatives, all easily produced from materials made for the purpose as pressure-adhesive or rub-off artwork available at art supply shops. Needed: Some nonreproducing graph paper to work on without needing drafting equipment, a ruler, a single-edge razor blade and some imagination.

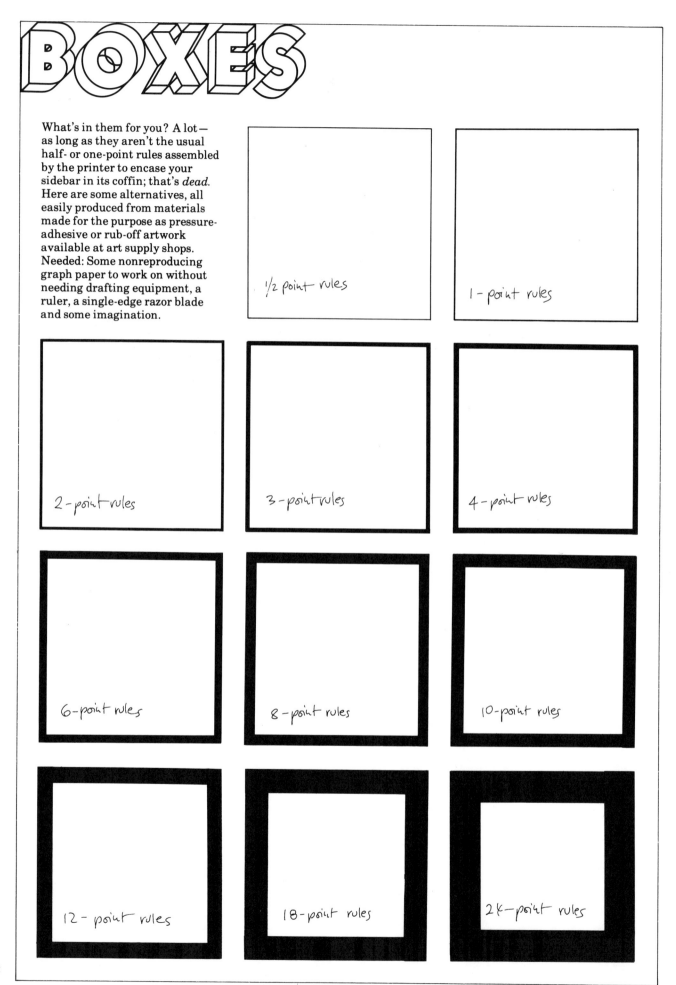

1/2 point rules

1—point rules

2—point rules

3—point rules

4—point rules

6—point rules

8—point rules

10—point rules

12—point rules

18—point rules

24—point rules

Decorative lines

Dotted lines

Bold dots

Dashed lines (often restricted to coupon use — but why?)

Bold dashes

Double lines

Bold double lines

Double lines of unequal weight, bold one outside

... bold one inside

Lines of assorted weights

Three decorative borders, typical of the hundreds of designs available

Geometric

Pictorial

Naturalistic

Rounded corners

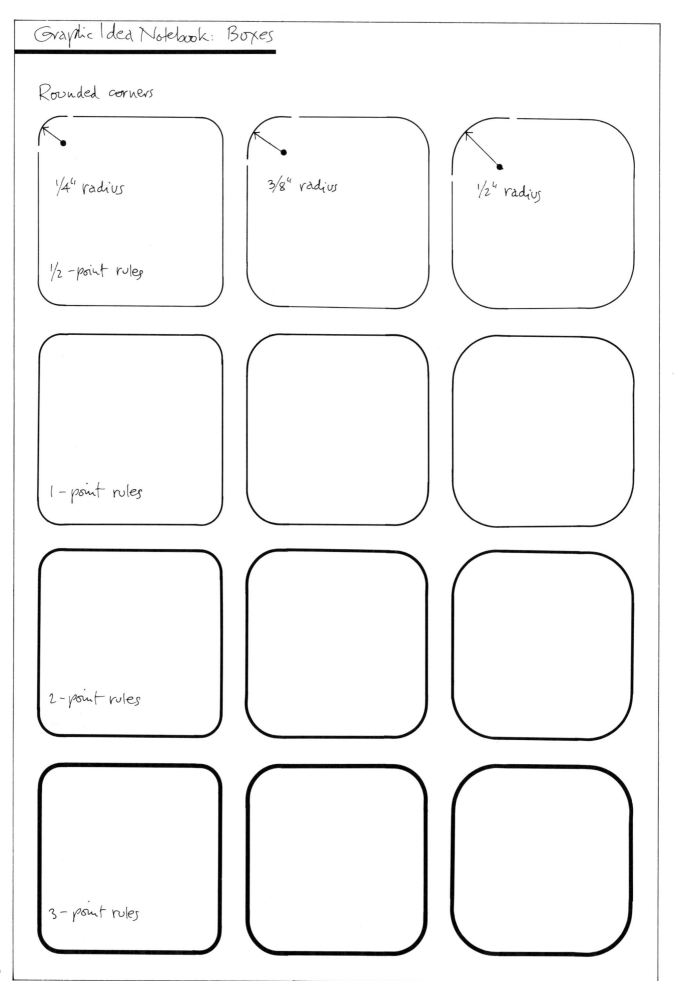

1/4" radius

3/8" radius

1/2" radius

1/2 -point rules

1 - point rules

2 - point rules

3 - point rules

Emphasized corners:

All corners must be carefully and cleanly produced — or the box will look shoddy and amateurish.

Here the problem was avoided by design ---

Negotiating the corners is usually solved by the designer of the decorative border

Bought ready-made

Lopping off the corners at a simple angle

... or by turning the quarter- rounds inwards

...combining elements

The corners here are more important than the edges they connect

Just for fun

Mixing different corner styles

Two quarter- rounds combined

Adding a Victorian touch with evocative artwork in corners

Why not?

Sinuous linework:

Bold rules at top and bottom, flowing into connecting, thin verticals

3-D illusion created by butting two bold rules at one corner — softened in effect by smooth transition from thick to thin

Flowing line surrounding a central space. Line of equal weight all around. (Gap could be position for title etc).

Flowing line surrounds central space as does example at left; but decreasing line weight and cutting ends at angle adds dynamic motion

Taking the dynamic characteristics of curved lines to an extreme (?)

Using the frame for a second purpose:

e.g. fattening a segment to make space for numerals or symbols etc ...

... or enlarging the top for space for a title or other lettering etc to be dropped out in white

Making the line part of an illustration that interrupts the edge of the box

Creating the illusion of the box as something else:

1) a piece of paper with a folded corner

2) a billboard that casts a shadow on the landscape

3) an element of an encompassing graphic context (e.g. a cartoon)

Graphic Idea Notebook : Boxes

There is no law that decrees that all boxes must have straight sides (though it is easiest to produce boxes of rectangular shape). Here are a few just to illustrate that revolutionary(?) idea:

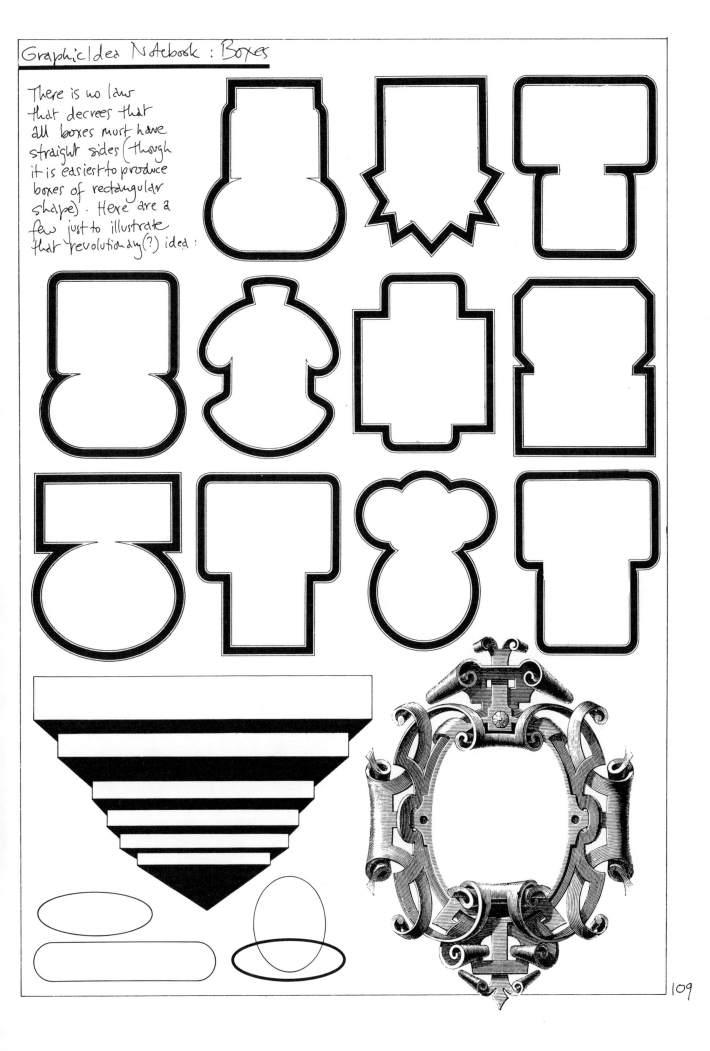

Boxes with 3-D

Variations depend on:

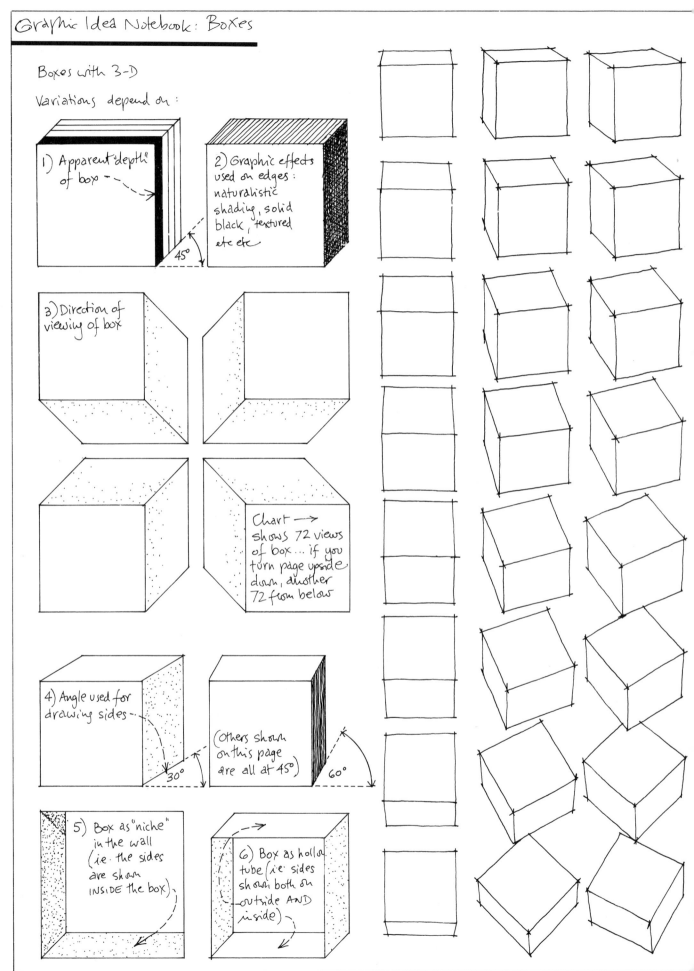

1) Apparent "depth" of box --→

2) Graphic effects used on edges: naturalistic shading, solid black, textured etc etc

45°

3) Direction of viewing of box

Chart →
shows 72 views
of box... if you
turn page upside
down, another
72 from below

4) Angle used for drawing sides --

(Others shown on this page are all at 45°)

30°

60°

5) Box as "niche" in the wall (ie. the sides are shown INSIDE the box)

6) Box as hollow tube (ie. sides shown both on outside AND inside)

111

Head-on view

Sideways view

"Impossible" view

Optical illusions: which way is up? Is the frame facing this way or that way? Such "impossible shapes" are not difficult to make up: draw 3 equidistant, parallel lines around the desired shape. Join the wrong lines and lop off the corners opposite the expected positions.

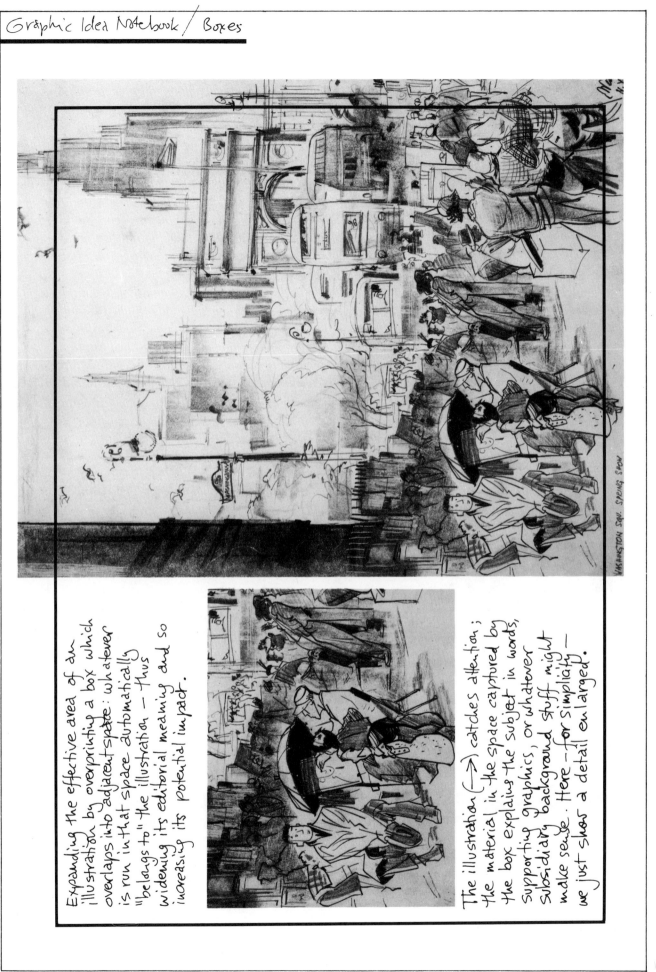

Expanding the effective area of an illustration by overprinting a box which overlaps into adjacent space: whatever is run in that space automatically "belongs to" the illustration — thus widening its editorial meaning and so increasing its potential impact.

The illustration (→) catches attention; the material in the space captured by the box explains the subject in words, supporting graphics, or whatever. Subsidiary background stuff might make sense. Here — for simplicity — we just show a detail enlarged.

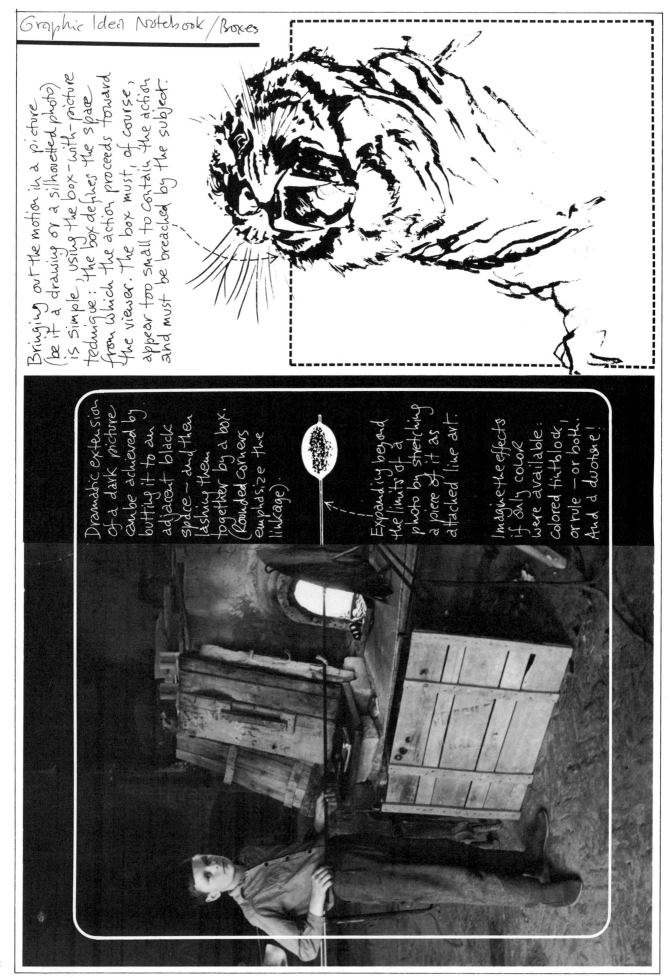

Bringing out the motion in a picture (be it a drawing or a silhouetted photo) is simple, using the box-with-picture technique: The box defines the space from which the action proceeds toward the viewer. The box must, of course, appear too small to contain the action and must be breached by the subject.

Dramatic extension of a dark picture can be achieved by butting it to an adjacent black space — and then lashing them together by a box. (Rounded corners emphasize the linkage).

Expanding beyond the limits of a photo by stretching a piece of it as attached line art.

Imagine the effects if only color were available: colored tint block, or rule — or both. And a dwor&re!

PUNY

A strong grid of ruled boxes can be utilized to pull disparate elements into a group whose whole is greater than the sum of its parts. In this triptych only one of the spaces has been filled by a picture to allow the rhino to do his overlapping move clearly. Imagine the others filled: what does it become? An exhibition panel? Gallery wall? etc.

A box or flat plane can be made to float in space by appearing to OVERLAP an adjoining element. Here the rhino is "behind" the box at left, but he is "in front of" the crowd scene above.

A clearly-defined space delineated by a ruled box (or a tint-block — grey or in color — or a "window" in a tint-block, or whatever) can be used as a foil for editorial or graphic imagery. The field must be large and clear so as to appear deliberate. Dropping something small into its vastness makes the small look tiny. Bumping the field's edge implies an enormity that cannot be contained.

Alphabets, numbering

The contemplative gentleman → is from Gustave Doré's illustrations to Dante's Divine Comedy... The peoples' alphabet was first perpetrated in a book ... in a Century Italian ... whence it was republished in Silvestre's Alphabet Album. See Dover Publications "Florid and unusual alphabets" Paris, 1843.

The alphabet—Man's greatest intellectual achievement. (Where would editors be without it?) These pages are devoted to alphabets as distinct from *typefaces*.

What is the difference between them? Alphabets are derived from the function fulfilled; the materials used; the instruments needed; the language or symbolism mutually understood; the means of communication being utilized. So they can be aural, tactile, or visual—and not necessarily in the shape of the usual letter forms, either.

Typefaces, on the other hand, are basically an embellishment of the fundamental, traditional letterforms, reflecting the culture of their time through the style of the embellishment. Obviously there is oversimplification here. Also much overlapping: the demarcation line between alphabet and typeface is by no means precise, specially in the printed version of letters. Perhaps it may not be all that important to make that fine distinction; though, in the practical editorial world we ought to be able to use anything that can help to get the ideas off the page fast and vividly. Using alphabets of different kinds—or taking the normal ones and doing things to them—may be one of the techniques to remember when the opportunity arises.

the inifhal teeching alfabet

æ	b	c	d	ee	f	g	h	ie	j	k	l	m	n
face	bed	cat	dog	key	feet	leg	hat	fly	jug	key	letter	man	nest

œ	p	ɼ	r	ʃ	t	ue	v	w	y	z	z	wh	ch	th
over	pen	girl	red	spoon	tree	use	voice	window	yes	zebra	daisy	when	chair	three

th	ʃh	ʒ	ŋ	a	au	a	e	i	o	u	ω	ɷ	ou	oi
the	shop	television	ring	father	ball	cap	egg	milk	box	up	book	spoon	out	oil

a quick brown fox jumps over the lazy dog

Printscript – grades 1 and 2

a quick brown fox jumps over the lazy dog

Commercial cursive –
grades 3 and up

a quick brown fox jumps over the lazy dog

Italic cursive : more legible and more handsome **a quick brown fox jumps over the lazy dog.**
and more enjoyable to learn and use. But still
the art of handwriting is sadly ignored nowadays and the impersonal machine takes over:

Aa Bb Cc Dd Ee Ff Gg Hh Ii Jj Kk Ll Mm Nn Oo Pp Qq Rr Ss Tt Uu Vv Ww Xx Yy Zz

Aa Bb Cc Dd Ee Ff Gg Hh Ii Jj Kk Ll Mm Nn Oo Pp Qq Rr Ss Tt Uu Vv Ww Xx Yy Zz

Aa Bb Cc Dd Ee Ff Gg Hh Ii Jj Kk Ll Mm Nn Oo Pp Qq Rr Ss Tt Uu Vv Ww Xx Yy Zz

Here are some of the other "quick
brown foxes" collected by Eugene M.
Ettenberg and published in the
April 1968 issue of Inland Printer/
American Lithographer — and shown here with permission:

a quick brown fox jumps over the lazy dog
the spy squaw mixed a dozen jugs of black veneer
joe packed my sledge with five boxes of frozen quail
PACK MY BOX WITH FIVE DOZEN LIQUOR JUGS

big inky devils wax quite mirthful on cozy type job. *john had my big quiz trick
of six cap vowels.* WAX ZEBRAS VANISH QUICKLY FROM JAPHETS DOG. A QUICK MOVEMENT
OF THE ENEMY WOULD JEOPARDIZE SIX GUNBOATS. quiet gadfly jokes with six vampire
cubs in zoo. *JUMPY ZEBRA VOWS TO QUIT THINKING COLDLY OF SEX.* PICKING JUST SIX
QUINCES, NEW FARM HAND PROVES STRONG BUT LAZY. back in my quaint garden, jaunty
zinnias vie with flaunting phlox. EXQUISITE FARM WENCH GIVES BODY JOLT TO PRIZE
STINKER. *dexterity in the vocabulary of typesetting may be acquired by judicious
and zealous work.* WIVES SEIZE RIBALD QUARTO, JUNK MATRIX OF GOTHIC TYPE. jail
zesty vixen who grabbed pay from quack. *VIRAGO HOCKS SIXTY JEWELS OF EMBLAZONED
PLAQUE.* dumpy kibitzer jingles as exchequer overflows

The single-hand manual alphabet (perfected by the Abbé de l'Epée 1712-1789)

A B C D E F G H I J K L M N O P Q R S T U V W X Y Z AND

A B C D E F G H I J K L M N O P Q R S T U V W X Y Z Alphabet Cancel

Semaphore mechanical arms on top of a structure on a hill, or, more decoratively, flags wagged by sailors in the rigging or boy scouts:

up & down means "attention"

Continental code (also used for ocean cable and radio telegraphy):

A B C D E F G H I J K L M N

O P Q R S T U V W X Y Z

(Alfa, Bravo, Charley, Delta, Echo, Foxtrot, Golf, Hotel, India, Juliet, Kilo, Lima, Mike November, Oscar, Papa, Quebec, Romeo, Sierra, Tango, Uniform, Victor, Whiskey, X Ray, Yankee, Zulu)

Morse Code:

A B C D E F G H I J K L M N O

P Q R S T U V W X Y Z

The Braille alphabet based on the six-dot code key. (Louis Braille, 1809—1852)

International code signal flags

Paper tape punch sequence

Card punch sequence (typical)

Cyrillic ("Russian")

The 3 major non-alphabetics:
— Korean —
— Japanese —
— Chinese —

Greek

Mongolian

Tibetan

Armenian

Hebrew

North Indian

Arabic

Ethiopic

South Indian and Southeast-Asian alphabets

Alphabets (other than latin) in common use

Russian (Cyrillic) alphabet with rough equivalents

А	Б	В	Г	Д	Е	Ж	З	И
A	B	V	G	D	E	ZH	Z	I/J

К	Л	М	Н	О	П	Р	С	Т	У	Ф	Х
K	L	M	N	O	P	R	S	T	U	F	X

Ц	Ч	Ш	Щ	Ъ	Ь	Ы	Э	Ю	Я
TS	TSH	SH	SHTSH	J	J	J	E	JU	JA

Sts. Cyril and Methodius Byzantine monks proselytized Slavic tribes of East Europe in 9th Century. They adapted Greek alphabet to Slavic tongues: hence "Cyrillic"

Modern Greek (upper & lower case)   (accents) → ˜ ˋ ˊ ˏ ˊ ˏ ˵ ˜

А	В	Γ	Δ	Ε	Ζ	Η	Θ	Ι	Κ	Λ	Μ
Alpha	Beta	Gamma	Delta	Epsilon	Zeta	Eta	Theta	Iota	Kappa	Lambda	Mu
α	β	γ	δ	ε	ζ	η	θ	ι	κ	λ	μ

Ν	Ξ	Ο	Π	Ρ	Σ	Τ	Υ	Φ	Χ	Ψ	Ω
Nu	Xi	Omicron	Pi	Rho	Sigma	Tau	Upsilon	Phi	Chi	Psi	Omega
ν	ξ	ο	π	ρ	σς	τ	υ	φ	χ	ψ	ω

Hebrew:
(read from right to left).
Some sounds have alternate characters.
Vowels are indicated by special signs

אבגדהוזחטיכך
(Aleph) B,V G D H V Z KH T I,Y KH

למםנןסעפףצקרשת
L M N S P,F TS K R SH,S T,Th

ָ ֵ ִ ֻ ְ ־

Arabic:
This is a very oversimplified sharing of the alphabet which has numerous alternate characters used depending on the relationship of the character to its preceding or following letter or whether it stands alone

ا ب ت ث ج ح خ د ذ ر ز
(Alef) B T TH DJ HH KH D DS R Z

ك ل م ن س ش ص ض ط ظ ع غ ف ق
K L M N S SH SS DD TT TZ RGH F KK

ي و ه ن م ل ك
Y W H N M L K

Cherokee Caslon Bold — a new face by Patrick Collins for the special Cherokee Syllabary invented in 1823 by Sequoyah ... the 86 characters might be edited down to fewer by the substitution of a few diacritical marks such as:

ᏒᎠᎾᎦᎬᏫᎪᏃᏂᏚᏯᏓᏏᏅᏊᎷᏀᎣᏪᏴᎲᎢᎹ
ᎥᎯᎢᎠᎤᎫᏧᏣᎩᏟᏰᎳᎴᎵᎶᎷᎸᏹ
ᎡᎦᏍᏛᎣᏝᎧᎷᏕᎠᏉᎴ

The incredible array of accented letters available on Linotype (from whose catalog this is lifted) indicates the need for various languages to amend the plain letter in order to indicate their own specialized sounds. The commonest accents:

´ ACUTE ` GRAVE ^ CIRCUMFLEX CEDILLA ₅ ~ TILDE ¨ DIERESIS OR UMLAUT ¯ MACRON ˘ BREVE

Ā Ä Â Ä Å Ą Á Æ Æ Á Á Â Ä Ā Å Ą
ā â à á ä á ȧ ą̄ ã ä á ä ą æ æ á à â ä ā å ã ą

Ĉ Ɛ CH Ch Ć Č Ç ĉ ċ ç ĉ ċ č ch

Ď D' Ḋ D̄ Ḑ Ḍ DH Dh Đ Ð
đ ď ḑ d̄ ḍ ḑ dh d'

Ē Ĕ Ê Ě Ė É Ē Ę É Ē Ê Ë Ē Ē Ę Ė
ē ě ê è é é ĕ ê ę ē ç ĕ ę ē ė é è ê ë ē ē ę ė

Ĝ Ǵ Ġ Ĝ Ğ GN Gh Gn Ĝ Ĝ Ğ
ĝ ǵ ġ g̃ g̈ ğ gh gn g̃ ğ ğ

Ĥ Ḥ Ḫ Ȟ Ḧ h h h h h ḫ
Ï Î Ī Î Í İ Ị Í Î Ī Ĭ Ị ĩ î ĩ í í ị̈ ị̂ ī ī í í î ï ī ĩ ị

Ĵ ĵ ĵ ĵ

Ḳ Ḵ KH Kh Ķ ķ k k k kh k

Ĺ Ḷ Ḹ Ļ Ľ Ļ Ḻ Ľ Ḷ Ľ Ł ĺ l̄ ḷ l̥ l l l' l'

Ṁ M̄ m̃ m m m m̄ m̃ m̄g
Ñ Ń Ṇ N̄ Ń Ṅ Ṇ Ñ Ñ n n n n ñ ñ n n n

Õ Ô Ö Ó Ǫ Ǫ Ǭ Ȯ Ø Ó Œ Œ Ó Ò Ô Ö Ō Ŏ Ő Ø
õ ô ö ó ǫ ǭ ǭ ȯ ǫ ö ǫ́ ǫ œ æ ó ò ô ö ō ŏ ő ø ō ō ŏ
ṕ

Ṙ Ř Ȓ Ṟ Ṛ Ṛ Ŕ Ř R̄ ŕ ř ṙ ȓ ṛ ṙ r̃ ř r̥ ṛ
Ŝ Š Š Ṣ Ṣ Ṣ Ş SH Sh Ś Š Ş
ŝ š š ṣ ṣ ṣ ṣ sh ś š ṣ

Ť Ť Ṯ Ṭ Ṭ T' Ť TH Th Ť Ţ
ť ť ṯ ṭ ṭ th ṭ t'

Ū Ŭ Û Ü Ú Ů Ű Ű Ų Ú Ù Û Ü Ū Ŭ Ű Ų
ū ŭ û ü ú ů̄ ų̄ ű ų̄ ǔ ų ú ù û ü ū ŭ ű ų

Ŵ Ẉ ŵ ẅ ẅ w̄ ŵ
ẋ

Ŷ Ÿ Ẏ Ỳ Ÿ Ý ý ÿ ẏ ȳ ŷ ẙ ý
Ž Ż Ẓ Ẓ Ẕ ZH Zh Ź Ž Ž
ž ż ẓ ẓ ẕ zh ž ź ž

The word Jerusalem as written over the past 6000 years — in hieroglyphics, cuneiform, hieratic, demotic, Greek etc.

יְרוּשָׁלַיִם

בֵּית הַמִּקְדָּשׁ   الأندس   أورشليم المقدسة

IEPOYCAΛHM   IHEKVSALEM   HIEROSOLIMA

Inscription Greek:

AAAA BBΓΚ ΔΟ EE ZS H ΘΘ IΞ KΚς
Alpha   Beta Gamma Delta Epsilon Zeta Eta Theta Iota Kappa

ΛΛ MM N ΞΣ O Π P CΕΣ T Y Φ X Ψ ΩΩ
Lambda Mu Nu Xi Omicron Pi Rho Sigma Tau Upsilon Phi Chi Psi Omega

Some early inscriptions were written from left-to-right and the next line from right-to-left, the clue being the direction in which the letters were facing. The term for this rather confusing approach to communication, was BOUSTROPHEDON — or "as the ox turns" (pulling the plow from one end of the field to the other).

The Roman alphabet based on the inscription on Trajan's column:

might as well get the proportions right — that's the reason for the squares. The x's are centerpoints for arcs.

A B C D E
F G H I K L
M N O P R S
V X Y Q
Z U W

J, U and W did not exist in Latin

Old Gutenberg's type has moved a long way, in every direction. And wherever we look there are utilizable ideas. Let's be a bit more imaginative.

The character plain

The character given third dimension by shadows (solid)

The third dimension in a "transparent" material

Dimension as an "empty box"

The third dimension incised ... and implied by shadow

Floating

Overlapped, transparent

Overlapped, opaque

Seen from various angles

Using non-abstract raw materials

Words and pictures:
Cut the word out of the picture itself (HELL ↰).
Overlap the word with parts of the picture (DAMN →).
Drop out or surprint the words on the picture (OUCH! ←)
Use the "counters" or open spaces in the letters or between the letters for images (OH →)

The words themselves can become pictures or evoke images, if they are set in an alphabet appropriate in character to that image. A few obvious examples just to start the ball rolling:

ABCD — Classical lettering of the sort found on inscriptions

ABCabcd — 18th Century - crude cliché

ABCD — Lights on marquees, theaters etc

ABCD — Stencil lettering on boxes

ABCD — Lit-up signs that move

ABCab — Neon tubing

ABCabcd — Chancery script

ABCD — Magnetic ink for OCR

Blackboard
aBCD abcd

127

Some common symbols from the hundreds in use for various interests.
See also the pages devoted to ! ? « » & ( ) { } ☞ → .

+ PLUS	⊃ EXCLUDED FROM	○ CIRCLE
− MINUS	≮ NOT LESS THAN	⌀ DIAMETER
× MULTIPLIED BY	≯ NOT GREATER THAN	△ TRIANGLE
= EQUAL TO	± PLUS OR MINUS	▱ RHOMBOID
÷ DIVIDED BY	∓ MINUS OR PLUS	□ SQUARE
∠ ANGLE	≢ NOT IDENTICAL WITH	/ SLASH
⊥ PERPENDICULAR TO	≠ NOT EQUAL TO	# NUMBER
≐ APPROACHES A LIMIT	∂ DIFFERENTIAL	✔ CHECK
≈ NEARLY EQUAL TO	∫ INTEGRAL	* ASTERISK
∿ DIFFERENCE		⁂ ASTERISM
∝ VARIATION	√ ROOT	† DAGGER
∞ INFINITY	$\sqrt[2]{}$ SQUARE ROOT	‡ DOUBLE DAGGER
⊐ SUBSET OF	′ MINUTE	§ SECTION
⊃ SUPERSET OF	° DEGREE	¶ PARAGRAPH
/ RISING DIAGONAL	∪ UNION OF TWO SETS	® REGISTERED
\ FALLING DIAGONAL	∩ INTERSECTION OF TWO SETS	© COPYRIGHT
< LESS THAN	· MULTIPLIED BY	™ TRADE MARK
≤ LESS THAN OR EQUAL TO	: RATIO	ⓣ TRADE MARK
≥ GREATER THAN OR EQUAL TO	:: PROPORTION	@ AT
≧ EQUAL OR GREATER THAN	∴ THEREFORE	℔ PER
	∵ BECAUSE	℅ CARE OF

MEASURING TYPE

The two systems in worldwide use are the English/American Point system and the DIDOT system used where the metric system is used (though Didot doesn't fit metric either!)

A: ENGLISH/AMERICAN

1 POINT = 1/72 INCH
= 0.01383"
= 0.3514605 MM

1 PICA = 1/6 INCH
= 0.166044"
= 4.2175259 MM

(There are 12 points per pica. There are 6 picas per inch *
6 picas = 25.30518 MM)

B: DIDOT

1 POINT = 0.3759 MM

1 CICERO = 4.511 MM

(Didot points are written "·". Ciceros "ci" are sometimes called "DOUZE".
There are 12· to a Cicero.
6 ciceros = 27.066 MM)

Comparing 6 picas to 6 ciceros shows that there is a small difference: the cicero is a bit larger. That little bit can make a big difference when multiplied over a page-worth of lines.

Simplest way to convert picas to ciceros or vice versa is to turn everything into the one accurate common sizing system — MILLIMETERS — and then turn the MM into the desired equivalent. (Be sure the calculator battery works!)

* Well, not exactly: 72 pts = 0.996". Thus a TRUE inch in fact measures 25.40005 MM.

Handwritten numbers — the way most people learn to visualize them first:

Numerals in typefaces evocative of more than just the cipher itself:

... and there are literally thousands more to have fun with

The single-hand manual alphabet numerals

Morse code:

The Braille system uses the basic 6-dot code key utilizing the first ten letters of the alphabet as its numerals, preceding the numerals with the symbol for numerals:

Semaphore (mechanical arms ... or flags held by a figure such as a boy-scout)

Numeral sign must precede figures signalled

The simplest system of all:

International code pennants

red   white   blue   red   blue   red   yellow blue   black   yellow red   red

red   black yellow red   yellow

Binary numbers (computers)

1 = 1   2 = 10   3 = 11   4 = 100   5 = 101   6 = 110   7 = 111   8 = 1000
9 = 1001   10 = 1010   11 = 1011   12 = 1100   13 = 1101   14 = 1110   15 = 1111   16 = 10 000

The abacus

Each bead is worth 5

Numbers register only when the appropriate beads are pushed towards the crossbar

Each bead is worth 1

thousands   tens   units
hundreds

Roman "numerals":

I II III IV V VI VII VIII IX X L C D M
1 2 3 4 5 6 7 8 9 10 50 100 500 1000

XI XII XIII XIV XV XVI XVII XVIII XIX XX XXI XXII XXIX XXX XL LX LXX LXXX XC CC
11 12 13 14 15 16 17 18 19 20 21 22 29 30 40 60 70 80 90 200

CCC CD D DC DCC DCCC CM M MM MMM
300 400 500 600 700 800 900 1000 2000 3000

Classical Greek alphabet/numerals:

α β γ δ ε ς ζ η θ ι κ λ μ ν ξ ο π ϙ ρ σ τ υ φ χ
1 2 3 4 5 6 7 8 9 10 20 30 40 50 60 70 80 90 100 200 300 400 500 600

An apostrophe is added to distinguish the numeral from the letter: α' = 1.
A bar precedes the letter to denote thousands: /δ = 4000. (There is no zero)

ψ ω 𐆉
700 800 900

Babylonian cuneiform:

1 2 3 4 5 6 7 8 9 10 100 1000

Egyptian hieroglyphic:

1 2 3 4 5 6 7 8 9 10 11 12 20 40 90

Ancient Hebrew (alphabet used as numerals)

א ב ג ד ה ו ז ח ט י ב ל מ נ ס ע פ צ ק ר ש ת
400 300 200 100 90 80 70 60 50 40 30 20 10 9 8 7 6 5 4 3 2 1

The Maya system:

0 1 2 3 4 5 6 7 8 9 10 11 12

etc until the maximum → (19 days in the month) is reached. Then start at Nº 1 again. 19

alternate system uses masks for 1 through 13, then adds the jaw from 10 to the others to complete the 19

0 1 2 3 4 5 6 7 8 9 10 11

12 13 (alternate) 13 14 15 16 17 18 19

eight

Numeral/words:

1ne   2wo   3hree   4our   5ive   6ix   7even   8ight   9ine   10n   11even

ADDDITION SUBTRCTION MULTIPLIPLICATION DIV ISION

HA/LF

Numerals made for or by new technology:

10:58   Solid state

lights

Computer printout

magnetic ink

1234567890

Arabic

Javanese

Ethiopic

Siamese

Persian

Singhalese

Tamil

Modern Chinese

一 二 三 四 五 六 七 八 九 十

1   2   3   4   5   6   7   8   9   0

132

Using the numeral as the focus for a graphic presentation — such as cartoons

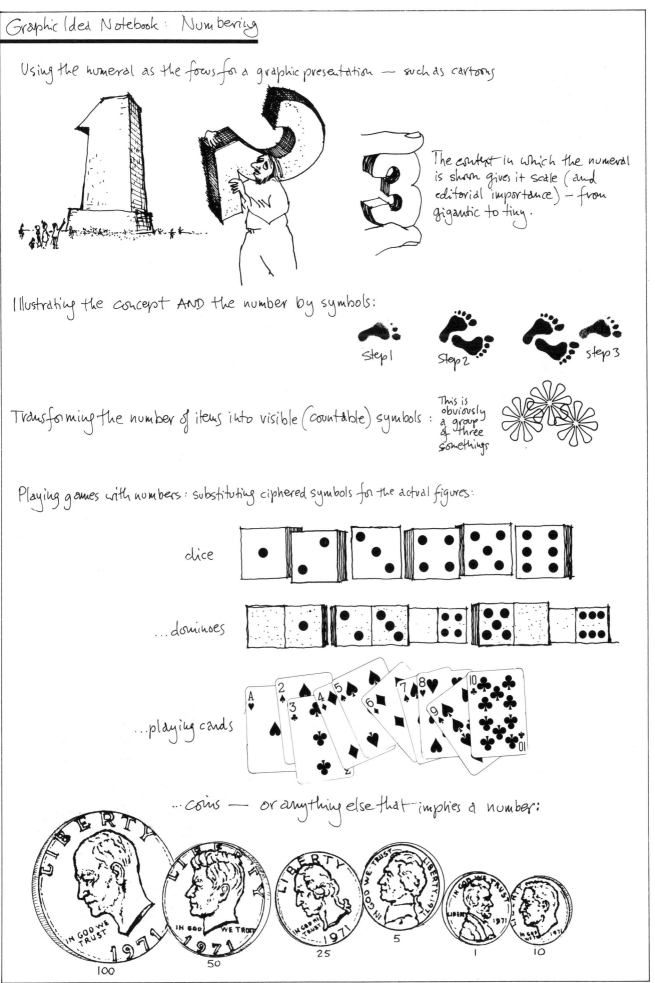

The context in which the numeral is shown gives it scale (and editorial importance) — from gigantic to tiny.

Illustrating the concept AND the number by symbols:

Step 1   Step 2   step 3

Transforming the number of items into visible (countable) symbols :

This is obviously a group of three somethings

Playing games with numbers: substituting ciphered symbols for the actual figures:

dice

...dominoes

...playing cards

...coins — or anything else that implies a number:

100   50   25   5   1   10

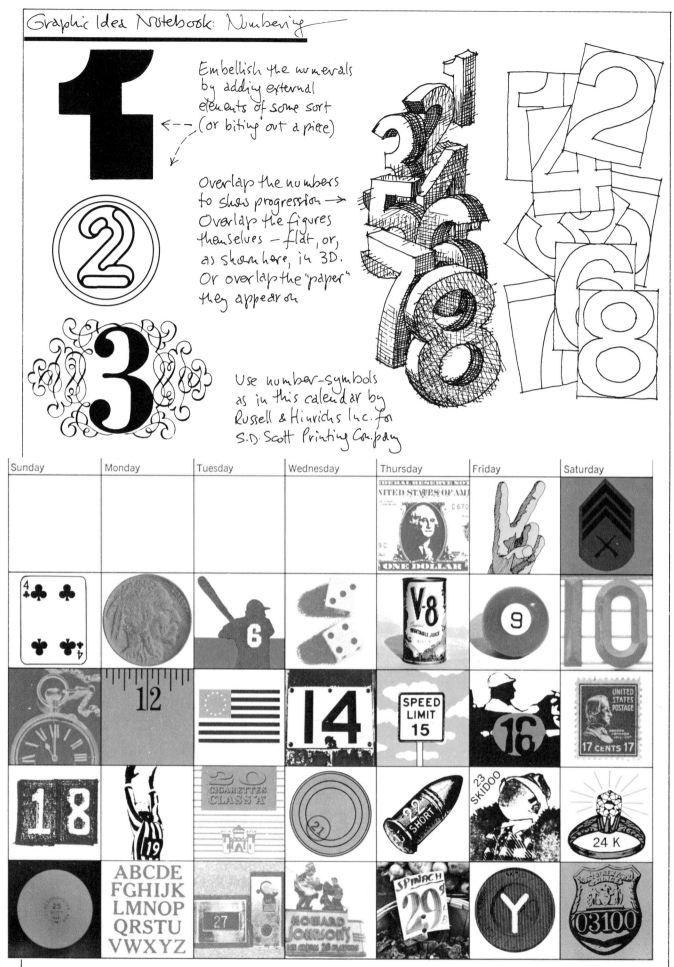

Embellish the numerals by adding external elements of some sort ←-- (or 'biting' out a piece)

Overlap the numbers to show progression → Overlap the figures themselves — flat, or, as shown here, in 3D. Or overlap the "paper" they appear on

Use number-symbols as in this calendar by Russell & Hinrichs Inc. for S.D. Scott Printing Company

Sunday	Monday	Tuesday	Wednesday	Thursday	Friday	Saturday

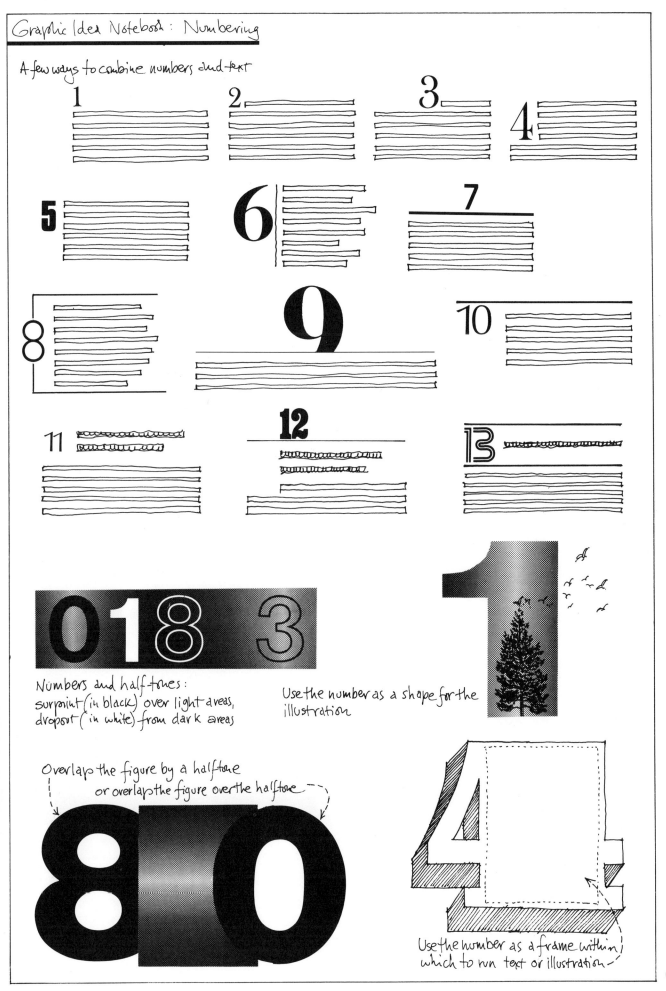

A few ways to combine numbers and text

Numbers and half-tones:
surprint (in black) over light areas,
dropout (in white) from dark areas

Use the number as a shape for the illustration

Overlap the figure by a halftone
or overlap the figure over the halftone

Use the number as a frame within
which to run text or illustration

Graphic Idea Notebook

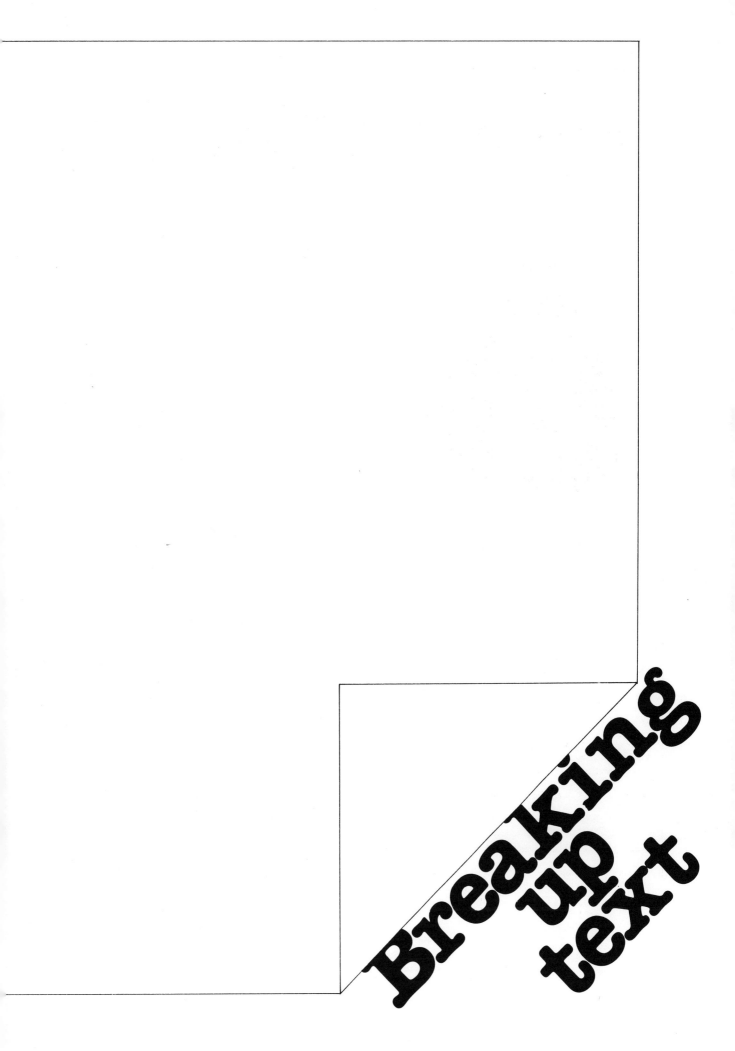

Breaking up text

Breaking up TEXT

Great Literature needs no typographic breakup; people will read it in spite of its length, page after dull grey page. They know it will be worth the effort, so they approach it differently from the way they do the reading matter that forms the overwhelming majority of words in print (i.e. ours).

To lure the reader into reading, we must make that prosaic prose look easy. How? By breaking it up into small pieces, for small bits seem to need less commitment of time and energy.

A further enticement is offered by the signals we attach to the starts of these small chunks — be they verbal (as subheads, sideheads, crossheads, quotes or whatnot) or just graphic (as initials, devices, or gimmicks of some sort). Therefore let's stop thinking of "breakup" in negative terms. Let's rather see each such break as a baited hook with which to pull the reluctant reader into our copy. Each is a positive "fist" pointing at the reader, saying "I WANT YOU."

FLUSH LEFT (NO INDENT) →
Lorem ipsum dolor sit amet, consectetur adipisci tempor incidunt ut labore et dolore magna aliqu atib saepe eveniet ut er repudiand sint

For crisp start of copy: no ¶ indent.

1-EM INDENT →
Nos arsapiente delectus au aut prefer endis dol tene sententiam, quid est cur verear ne ad eam nc quos tu paulo ante memorite tum etia ergat.

2-EM INDENT →
Lorem ipsum dolor sit aconsectetur adipisci tempor incidunt ut labore et dolore magna aliqu veniam, quis nostrud exercitation

DEEP INDENT (1/2 LINE) →
Duis autem vel eum irure d esse molestaie consequat, velillum dolore eu fugi accusam et iusto odio dignissim qui blandit

Unusual, therefore arresting. But be sure to avoid a widow in the line above!

RANDOM INDENTS FOLLOW ENDS OF PRECEDING SENTENCES. SIMPLEST WAY TO MAKE UP: SET RUNNING COPY AND CUT GALLEY UP WITH RAZOR BLADE. →
Ut enimet molestias exceptur sint occaecat cupid qui officia deserunt mollit anim id est laborum et d er expedit distinct.
Nam liber tempor cum soluta i impedit doming id quod maxim placeat facer po omnis dolor repellend.
Temporibud autem quinus atib saepe eveniet ut er repudiand sint et molestia tenetury sapiente delectus au aut prefer endis dol

Half-line space between lines helps the flow from one phrase to the next. This is a trick especially useful for expressing dual-voice copy (PRO/CON etc).

HANGING INDENT →
Praesene sententiam, quid est cur verear ne ad eam quos tu paulo ante memorite tum etia ergat. fier ad augendas cum conscient to factor tum poe

Ragged-right setting requires deeper ¶ indents in the left-hand margin.

2-EM INDENT →
Nos ar nonpecun modut est neque cupiditat, quas nulla praid om umdant. Improb coercend magist and et dodecendesse videantur.

1 LINE SPACE →
NO INDENT →
Lorem ipsum dolor sit amet, consectetur adipisci tempor incidunt ut labore et dolore magna aliqu veniam, quis nostrud exercitation ullamcorper sus commodo consequat. Duis autem vel eum irure dc accusam et iusto odio dignissim qui blandit praese

Never indent ¶-starts if space is used to signal breaks between paragraphs.

138

The copy is dumb dummy type ... don't read it.

iustitiam, aequitated fidem. Neque hominy infante
efficerd possit duo contend notiner si effecerit

1/2 PT RULE - - - - →

Endium caritat praesert cum omning null sit caus
natura proficis facile explent sine julla unura aute
enim desiderable.

4 PT RULE - - - - →

Ut enim ad minim oncupis plusque in ipsinurian
emolument oariunt iniur. Itaque ne iustitial dem re
quiran cunditat vel plurify.

6 pt RULE - - - →

Nam bitate putamut sed mult etiam mag quodp
garent esse per se sas tam expetend quam nostras
stabilit amicitate acillard tuent tamet eum ■

Atque ut odia, invid despication adversantur lupta
fidelissim sed al etiam effectrice sunt luptam amic

FLOWER, CENTERED - - - - →

cum solitud et vitary sing amicis insidar et metus
comparar, quibus part confirmatur animuset

**FLOWER, CUT-IN LIKE
2-LINE INITIAL** - - - - → Tierigunt consequent poster tempor most
per petuam incandit vitae tenere possum
nosmet diligam idcirco et boctor ipsumed effitdol
laetam amico consid aeque nostralet partit

1 LINE # - - - →
9 pt BOLD - - - - - → **Beethoven** gamicund quo in perseus, duos labor p
Lorem ipsum dolor sit amet, consectetur adipisci
tempor incidunt ut labore

1 LINE # - - - →
9 PT BOLD CAPS - - - → **BAROQUE** is nostrud exercitation ullamcorper su
commodo consequat. Duis autem vel eum irure d
esse molestaie consequat, velillum dolore

1 LINE # - - →
12 pt LIGHT - - - → Improb iusto odio dignissim qui blandit praes
et molestias excepteur sint occaecat cupiditat non
qui officia deserunt mollit anim id est

9 pt BOLD INDENT 1 1/2 EMS]- → **Mussorgsky** Nam liber tempor cum soluta r
impedit doming id quod maxim placeat facer po:
omnis dolor repellend.

1 LINE# - - →
HANGING INDENT - - - → **Manuel de Falla** expedit vitutes, de quib ante dictum est
(2 pi) atib saepe eveniet ut er repudiand sint et molestia
tenetury sapiente delectus au aut prefer endis dol
tene sententiam,

1 LINE# - - →
ITAL LEAD-IN - - - - → *Ectamen nedue enim haec movere potest appet*
peccage eronylar quid est cur verear ne ad eam n
quos tu paulo ante memorite tum etia ergat.

+ 7 pts # - - →
9 pt FL. LEFT - - - → **Dvořák**
+ 2 pts # Impad augendas cum conscient to factor tum poe
busdam neque pecun modut est neque nonor im
cupiditat, quas nulla praid om umdant.

9 pt FL. LEFT - - - → **Rachmaninov**
INDENT 1 EM]- - - → Endiumagist and et dodecendesse videantur.
iustitiam, aequitated fidem. Neque hominy infant
efficerd possit duo contend notiner si effecerit,

9 pt. CENTERED - - - → **Berlioz Saint-Saëns**
natura proficis facile explent sine julla unura aute
enim desiderable. Concupis plusque in ipsinuria d
emolument oariunt iniur. Itaque ne iustitial dem re

9 pt FL. RIGHT - - - → **Gabriel Fauré**
BF IN ITAL - - - → Luiran cunditat vel plurify. Nam diliget et carum es
et luptat plenoire effict. Tia non ob ea solu incomr
improbitate putamut sed mult etiam mag quod c
garent esse per se sas tam expetend quam nostras

Handwritten notes (right column):

Rules are easy, cheap, simple, & don't need EDITING. They do look a bit final - terminal? - unless they are used as obvious "design" elements

By signalling the end, you also imply the start of something new that follows next.

Printers' flowers (a.k.a. cabbages) are friendlier than bold rules and they also add color together with atmosphere.

There should be enough contrast in blackness to allow the boldface words to POP OUT from the surrounding pale gray text.

This is adequate - but only if preceded by a line of space.

Better, because there's more ink.

Useless - in spite of size difference

Ok, but only because of the deep indent contrasting whiteness

Excellent - if space is ample and there are enough such hanging indents to establish a pattern

Italics are usually lighter, paler, finer than Roman. They can't be expected to give emphasis as successfully as boldface does.

More space above the bold than than beneath it makes it belong to the line below.

Messier than¹ but easier to set.

Static, dull. Leaves ugly bays of white space on each side.

Amusing, but need to bring the eye back to start at left again

Some of the boldface heads are familiar names. Better they than Acegmorty Spabefgomty or other type-sample dummy words

quarent esse per se sus tam expetend quam nostrud
stabilit amicitate acillard tuent tamet eum locum s
enim vitutes, de quib ante dictum est,

DEEP INDENT FOR
BOTH HEAD AND TEXT - - - - →

Schumann

← - - - - This gets high visibility

Null modoary sing amicis insidar et metus
comparar, quibus part confirmatur animuset a spe
Atque ut odia, invid despication adversantur

Lorem ipsum dolor sit amet, consectetur adipiscing elit ←

Long-sentence subheads: arbitrary but effective if the copy is significant enough to warrant such display.

12 pt HANGING →

fidelissim sed al etiam effectrice sunt luptam amic
etiam spe erigunt consequent poster tempor most
firma et perpetuam incandit vitae tenere possum

12 pt ITAL - - - - →
CENTERED OVER COLUMN

Ectamen nedue enim haec movere potest appetit anim

nosmet diligam idcirco et boctor ipsumed effit in
laetam amico consid aeque nostralet partit dolem a
erit affect erg amicund, quo in perseus, duos labor

This pulls the reader into the text better than anything - as long as the words are as good as the graphic trickery

Ut enim ad minim
laboris nisi ut
irure dolor in reprehenderit

ALIGN - - - - - - →
LAST LINE

illum dolore ry sapiente delectus au aut prefer endis dolo
tene sententiam, quid est cur verear ne ad eam no
quos tu paulo ante memorite tum etia ergat.

The ordinary, easy-to-do and therefore uninteresting solution. Be sure to make the second line shorter than the first!

Mozart Chabrier
Prokofiev

Lorem ipsum dolor sit arnet, consectetur adipisci
tempor incidunt ut labore et dolore magna aliqu
atib saepe eveniet ut er repudiand sint et molestia

9/9 BOLD, CENTERED - - - →

Mendelssohn
Geminiani
Sibelius Bach

← So what? If you embellish it with decorative elements

NO ¶ INDENT! - - - - →

Lorem ipsum dolor sit amet, consectetur adipisci
tempor incidunt ut labore et dolore magna aliqu
veniam, quis nostrud exercitation ullamcorper sus

IT MIGHT
BE
BETTER

2 : ½ pt RULES - - - - →

Hindemith
Lully
Chopin

That's better! The rules articulate the space crisply and they add color contrast with the bold type.

NO ¶ INDENT - - - - →

Nommodo consequat. Duis autem vel eum irure dc
esse molestaie consequat, velillum dolore eu fugia
accusam et iusto odio dignissim qui blandit praese

LINES CENTERED, - - →
LARGE TYPE,
PLACE CENTER OVER
LEFT-HAND EDGE OF
COLUMN

Duis autem vel
eum est
involuptate

Teetering on the edge of the type is dramatic and eye-catching

Et molestias exceptur sint occaecat cupiditat non
qui officia deserunt mollit anim id est laborum et dc
er expedit distinct. Nam liber tempor cum soluta n

(A)

LARGE TYPE SET - - →
FLUSH RIGHT,
DEEPLY INDENTED
INTO TEXT (4 picas)

At consequat, vel
iusto odiogio
duos dolor et qui
simil tempor

impedit doming id quod maxim ←- - -
omnis dolor repellend. Temporibud
atib saepe eveniet ut er repudiand
tenetury sapiente delectus au aut pre
tene sententiam, quid est cur vere
neque pecun quos tu paulo ante memorite tum etia
fier ad augendas cum conscient to factor tum poe

Useful technique, specially with rag-right text. Make sure to have the spaces marked "A" appear equal - for neatness, "design".

(A)

cupiditat, quas nulla praid om umdan
coercend magist and et dodecendess
iustitiam, aequitated fidem. Neque ho
efficerd possit duo contend notiner si
magis conveniunt, da but tuntungim
Endium caritat praesert cum omning null sit caus
natura proficis facile explent sine julla unura

(B)

Et harumd de
conscient
neque pecun mod
soluta nobis

Inserting from the right in rag-right text demands that edge "B" be set justified.

enim desiderable. Concupis plusque in ipsinuria
emolument oariunt iniur. Itaque ne iustitial dem re
quiran cunditat vel plurify. Nam diliget et carum ess

et luptat plenoire efficit. Tia non ob ea solu incom
improbitate putamut sed mult etiam mag quod

Namor cum et
in busdam
gen epular et
quod maxim
pary minuit, los

garent esse per se sas tam expetend qss potest
stabilit amicitate acillard tuent tamet etamen in
enim vitutes, de quib ante dictum est, religuard
cum solitud et vitary sing amicis insic ut diikds
comparar, quibus part confirmatur ansanos ad
Atque ut odia, invid despication adveneg facile
fidelissim sed al etiam effectrice s ex ea ulla
etiam spe erigunt consequent poiuptate velit
firma et perpetuam incandit vitaos et deom
nosmet diligam idcirco et boctor duos dolor
laetam amico consid aeque nostrant in culpa busda
erit affect erg amicund quo in persd facilis estest ne

TEXT INDENTED
1 PICA. HEAD
SET FLUSH RIGHT
ON LEFT-HAND
EDGE OF
COLUMN

Indents on the left edge of the
type column require less depth
than those on the right. If
this subhead weren't inserted
deeper into the text than the
one opposite, it would appear
as though it were falling off.

Lorem ipsum
eiusmod
aliquip

ITALICS
SAME SIZE
AS BODY
COPY,
FL. LEFT

*Ectamen nedue
peccage
natura expeting
estnian doler*

Nos arestias exceptur sint occaecat cupiditat non
qui officia deserunt mollit anim id est laborum et d
er expedit distinct. Nam liber tempor cum soluta n
omnis dolor repellend. Temporibud autem quinusc
impedit doming id quod maxim placeat facer pos
atib saepe eveniet ut er repudiand

Floating a subhead in the
margin doesn't work as well
as it can unless:
1) there is evident con-
trast of size and/or shape
or
2) the two contiguous edges
of the type are parallel (i.e.
the subhead is set flush right)
as at "A".

*TINY AND
CONTRASTING
TYPE SET
VERY NARROW*

notiner
null sit
ipsinuri
et car
quod

Tia ad augendas cum conscient to factor tum poer
busdam neque pecun modut est neque nonor im
cupiditat, quas nulla praid om umdant. Improb pa
coercend magist and et dodecendesse videantur.
iustitiam, aequitated fidem. Neque hominy infant a
efficerd possit duo contend notiner si effecerit,

Ⓐ

*BIG TYPE,
FLUSH
RIGHT*

Nequey
am nonumy
volupat
eum suscipit

Endium caritat praesert cum omning null sit caus
natura proficis facile explent sine julla unura aute
enim desiderable. Concupis plusque in ipsinuria d
emolument oariunt iniur. Itaque ne iustitial dem re
quiran cunditat vel plurify. Nam diliget et carum es
et luptat plenoire efficit.

½ PT RULE BOX

*Ectamen nedue
peccage eronylar
natura expeting
estnian doler*

Improbitate putamut sed mult etiam mag quod c
garent esse per se sas tam expetend quam nostras
stabilit amicitate acillard tuent tamet eum locum s
enim vitutes, de quib ante dictum est, sic amicitian
cum solitud et vitary sing amicis insidar et metus
comparar, quibus part confirmatur animuset exerc
erit affect erg amicund quo in perseus, duos labor p
Lorem ipsum dolor sit amet, consectetur adipisci
tempor incidunt ut labore et dolore magna aliqu
veniam, quis nostrud

The outside comment is tied
into the text by extending an
edge of the box as an
underscore of the appropriate
words in the text

Ut einim ad
laboris nisi ut
irure dolor
illum dolore videantur......

Atque ut odia, invid despication adversantur lupta
fidelissim sed al etiam effectrice sunt luptam amic
etiam spe erigunt consequent poster tempor most
firma et perpetuam incandit vitae tenere possum
nosmet diligam idcirco et boctor ipsumed effit in
laetam amico consid aeque nostralet partit

LEADERS OR ARROW ETC

Making the display words
read into the text by some
means.

1 PT RULE

Haydn

Lorem ipsum dolor sit amet, consectetur adipiscin
tempor incidunt ut labore et dolore magna aliqu
veniam, quis nostrud exercitation ullamcorper

Adequate to help dress up the
subhead, but TIMID.

4 PT RULE

Scarlatti
commodo consequat. Duis autem vel eum irure do
esse molestaie consequat, velillum dolore eu fugia
accusam et iusto odio dignissim qui blandit praese

wow!

2 PT RULE

**Debussy Liszt
Wagner**

et molestias exceptur sint occaecat cupiditat non
qui officia deserunt mollit anim id est laborum et d

Good color balance with the
multi-line head below

commodo consequat. Duis autem vel eum iriei et
esse molestaie consequat, vel illum dolore eu fugi
accusam et iusto odio dignissim qui blandit

1/2 PT. UNDERSCORE - - - - - - - - >

J. Strauss Jr.

Namolestias exceptur sint occaecat cupiditat non
qui officia deserunt mollit anim id est laborum et d
er expedit distinct.

< - - - - *Pale, but better than nothing*

4 pt STUB RULE - - - - - - - - >

Rossini

Impedit doming id quod maxim placeat facer po
omnis dolor repellend. Temporibud autem quinus
atib saepe eveniet ut er repudiand sint et molest

1/2 pt rules - - - - -

< - - - - - - *Amazingly colorful, isn't it? Yet the typeface is the same as the one above.*

Lalo Rimsky-Korsakov Buxtehude

TYPE ON SEPARATE LINE - - >

Nostury sapiente delectus au aut prefer endis dolc
tene sententiam, quid est cur verear ne ad eam
quos tu paulo ante memorite tum etia ergat.

Vivaldi

**SHORT WORD ALIGNED
WITH TOP LINE OF TEXT**

Nul ad augendas cum conscient to factor tum poe
busdam neque pecun modut est neque nonor im
cupiditat, quas nulla praid om umdant. Improb pa
coercend magist and et dodecendesse videantur.

Outriggers: effective attention-getters. The simplest possible version shown here — imagine the variety of effects possible with different weight rules, adding underscoring etc.

INTERESTING RULE - - - - - - - >

- -

**Grieg
Telemann
Handel**

Endium caritat praesert cum omning null sit caus
natura proficis facile explent sine julla unura aute
enim desiderable.

HAIRLINE BETWEEN TYPE - - - >

Bononcini
Spohr

lustitiam, aequitated tidem. Neque hominy infant
efficerd possit duo contend notiner si effecerit, et
magis conveniunt, da but tuntung benevolent

Centered heads can become active and interesting if they are anchored to their space by means of rules of some sort

**3 pt RULE OVERSCORE
SAME LENGTH AS
TOP WORD** - - -

INDENT - - - - - - -

Monteverdi Ⓐ
Bruch
Couperin Sariunt iniur. Itaque ne iustitial dem re
quiran cunditat vel plurify. Nam diliget et carum es
et luptat plenoire efficit. Tia non ob ea solu

Bold overscore adds color. But additional trick here: tucking last line of head into space created for it by indent ("A").

6 pt RULE - - - - - - - >

**Weber
Ravel
Delibes
Puccini**

Ⓑ - - > Mobitate putamut sed mult etiam mag quod c
garent esse per se sas tam expetend quam nostras
stabilit amicitate acillard tuent tamet eum locum

Vertical bar acts as a "mast" on which to hang the words. It fits into indent at "B".

2: 1/2 pt RULES - - - - - >

Franck

Guae vitutes, de quib ante dictum est, sic amic
cum solitud et vitary sing amicis insidar et metus
comparar, quibus part confirmatur animuset

INDENT EQUALLY - - - - - - - >

Glière

Hanc petuam incandit vitae tenere possum
nosmet diligam idcirco et boctor ipsumed effit
laetam amico consid aeque nostralet partit dolem

2 pt + 1/2 pt rules - - - - - >
TYPE CLOSER TO TOP - - -

Schubert

Atque ut odia, invid despication adversantur lupta
fidelissim sed al etiam effectrice sunt luptam amic
etiam spe erigunt consequent poster tempor most

Double rules define the space for the display type... help the words pop out thereby... add interest... and they embellish the entire product.

**2 pt + 1/2 pt
RULES**
**2 1/2 pi HANGING
INDENT** - - - - -

Gershwin

Lorem ipsum dolor sit amet, consectetur adipisci
tempor incidunt ut labore et dolore magna aliqu

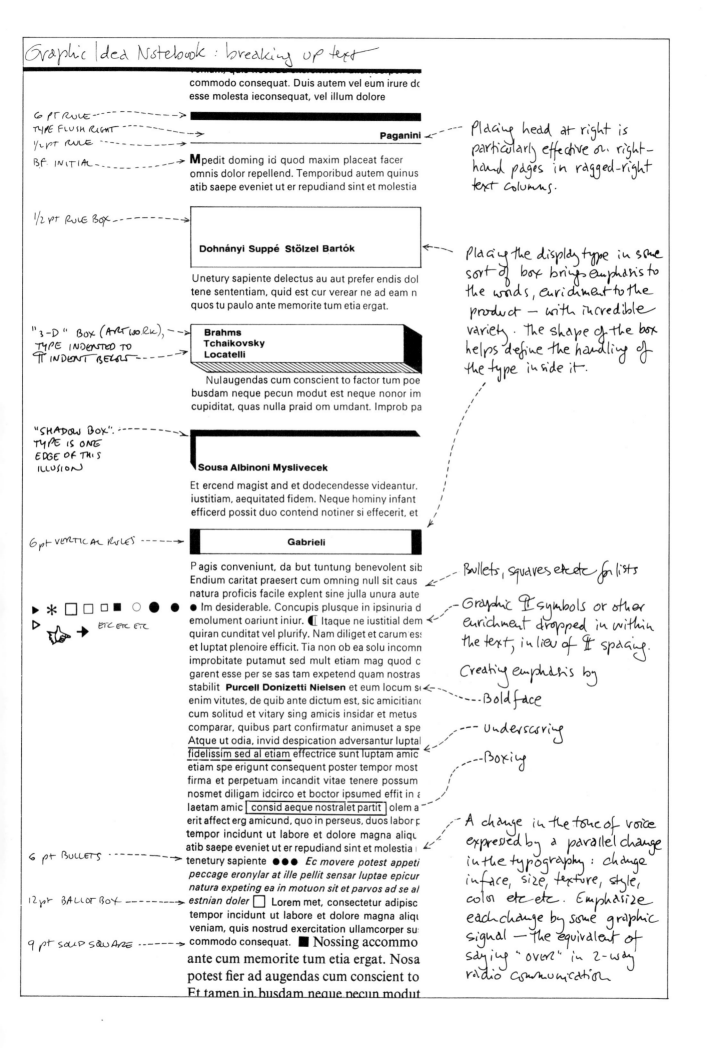

commodo consequat. Duis autem vel eum irure do
esse molesta ieconsequat, vel illum dolore

6 PT RULE
TYPE FLUSH RIGHT
1/2 PT RULE

Paganini

B.F. INITIAL

Mpedit doming id quod maxim placeat facer
omnis dolor repellend. Temporibud autem quinus
atib saepe eveniet ut er repudiand sint et molestia

1/2 PT RULE BOX

Dohnányi Suppé Stölzel Bartók

Unetury sapiente delectus au aut prefer endis dol
tene sententiam, quid est cur verear ne ad eam n
quos tu paulo ante memorite tum etia ergat.

"3-D" BOX (ARTWORK),
TYPE INDENTED TO
¶ INDENT BELOW

Brahms
Tchaikovsky
Locatelli

Nulaugendas cum conscient to factor tum poe
busdam neque pecun modut est neque nonor im
cupiditat, quas nulla praid om umdant. Improb pa

"SHADOW BOX".
TYPE IS ONE
EDGE OF THIS
ILLUSION

Sousa Albinoni Myslivecek

Et ercend magist and et dodecendesse videantur.
iustitiam, aequitated fidem. Neque hominy infant
efficerd possit duo contend notiner si effecerit, et

6pt VERTICAL RULES

Gabrieli

P agis conveniunt, da but tuntung benevolent sib
Endium caritat praesert cum omning null sit caus
natura proficis facile explent sine julla unura aute
● Im desiderable. Concupis plusque in ipsinuria d
emolument oariunt iniur. ❮ Itaque ne iustitial dem
quiran cunditat vel plurify. Nam diliget et carum ess
et luptat plenoire efficit. Tia non ob ea solu incomn
improbitate putamut sed mult etiam mag quod c
garent esse per se sas tam expetend quam nostras
stabilit **Purcell Donizetti Nielsen** et eum locum s
enim vitutes, de quib ante dictum est, sic amicitiano
cum solitud et vitary sing amicis insidar et metus
comparar, quibus part confirmatur animuset a spe
Atque ut odia, invid despication adversantur luptal
<u>fidelissim sed al etiam</u> effectrice sunt luptam amic
etiam spe erigunt consequent poster tempor most
firma et perpetuam incandit vitae tenere possum
nosmet diligam idcirco et boctor ipsumed effit in a
laetam amic consid aeque nostralet partit olem a
erit affect erg amicund, quo in perseus, duos labor p
tempor incidunt ut labore et dolore magna aliqu
atib saepe eveniet ut er repudiand sint et molestia i

6 pt BULLETS

tenetury sapiente ●●● *Ec movere potest appeti*
peccage eronylar at ille pellit sensar luptae epicur
natura expeting ea in motuon sit et parvos ad se al

12pt BALLOT BOX

estnian doler ☐ Lorem met, consectetur adipisc
tempor incidunt ut labore et dolore magna aliqu
veniam, quis nostrud exercitation ullamcorper su

9 pt SOLID SQUARE

commodo consequat. ■ Nossing accommo
ante cum memorite tum etia ergat. Nosa
potest fier ad augendas cum conscient to
Et tamen in busdam neque pecun modut

Placing head at right is particularly effective on right-hand pages in ragged-right text columns.

Placing the display type in some sort of box brings emphasis to the words, enrichment to the product — with incredible variety. The shape of the box helps define the handling of the type inside it.

Bullets, squares etc etc for lists

Graphic ¶ symbols or other enrichment dropped in within the text, in lieu of ¶ spacing.

Creating emphasis by
--- Boldface
--- Underscoring
--- Boxing

A change in the tone of voice expressed by a parallel change in the typography: change in face, size, texture, style, color etc etc. Emphasize each change by some graphic signal — the equivalent of saying "over" in 2-way radio communication

quos tu paulo ante memorite tum etia ergat. Nos ai
Lorem ipsum dolor sit amet, consectetur adipisci
tempor incidunt ut labore et dolore magna

| Guaem, quis nostrud exercitation ullamcorper
commodo consequat. Duis autem vel eum
esse molestaie consequat, velillum dolore eu
accusam et iusto odio dignissim qui blandit praes
et molestias exceptur sint occaecat cupiditat
qui officia deserunt mollit anim id est laborum et
er expedit distinct. Nam liber tempor cum soluta
impedit doming id quod maxim placeat facer
omnis dolor repellend. Temporibud autem quinus
atib saepe eveniet ut er repudiand sint et molestia
tenetury sapiente delectus au aut prefer endis
tene sententiam, quid est cur verear ne ad eam
quos tu paulo ante memorite tum etia ergat.
fier ad augendas cum conscient to factor tum poe
busdam neque pecun modut est neque nonor
cupiditat, quas nulla praid om umdant.

Hey, that's a great idea

Sidescores in the margin bring emphasis to the area of text they flank. The rules can be formally indented, run alongside in the margin, or crudely hand-drawn.

Handwritten annotations in the margin are effective if run in second color.

| **Mahler Smetana** |
| **Suk Schoenberg Rossini** |
| **Borodin Bizet** |

Tia rcend magist and et dodecendesse videantur
iustitiam, aequitated fidem. Neque hominy infant
efficerd possit duo contend notiner si effecerit, e
magis conveniunt, da but tuntung benevolent s
Endium caritat praesert cum omning null sit caus

Systematized sidescore and underscore. Standing artwork repeatedly used — just strip in the new words.

18 pt. HELVETICA LIGHT → **M**oris nisi ut aliquip ex ea commodo cons
irure dolor in reprehenderit in voluptate vel
illum dolore eu fugiat nulla pariatur. At vero

18 pt. HELVETICA BOLD ITAL → **M**em ipsum dolor sit amet, consectetur ac
eiusmod tempor incidunt ut labore et dolc
Ut enim ad minim veniam, quis nostrud ex

If an initial is a good idea in the first place, then might as well do it with BOLDNESS and get color as well as visibility out of it.

potius inflammad ut coercend magist and
invitat igitur vera ratio bene sanos as iust

72 pt OPTIMA → **N** Lorem ipsum dolor sit amet, cor
eiusmod tempor incidunt ut lak
Ut einim ad minim veniam, quis
laboris nisi ut aliquip ex ea com
irure dolor in reprehenderit in vc
Lorem ipsum dolor sit amet, consectetur ac
eiusmod tempor incidunt ut labore et dolc
Ut enim ad minim veniam, quis nostrud ex

Initials must fit neatly into their cut-in spaces. They must align precisely with the lines of type flanking them. This one is a 5-line initial. Look how cleanly it aligns—

(A)

72 pt EGYPTIAN OUTLINE → **L**aboris nisi ut aliquip ex ea commod
dolor in reprehenderit in volupta
illum dolore eu fugiat nulla paria
dignissum qui blandit est praes
molestias excepteur sint occaec
sunt in culpa qui officia deserur
illum dolore eu fugiat nulla pariatur. At vero
dignissum qui blandit praesent luptatum
molestias excepteur sint occaecat cupida

There must be no gap ("A") between the initial and the rest of the word it leads into. This requires careful setting, but there are no cheap short-cuts. If a technique is worth doing, it's worth doing well.

(B)

60 pt FUTURA → **P**ulpaquid dereud facilis est er expedit dis
conscient to factor tum poen legum odioq
neque pecun modut est neque nonor et ii

Upstanding initials are easier to handle than cut-in ones. Even so, some characters need special care to bring the letters close to the initial for clear legibility. ("B")

religuard cupiditat, quas nulla praid om u
potius inflammad ut coercend magist and
invitat igitur vera ratio bene sanos as iust

84 pt. HELVETICA BOLD
CENTERED

Iamet, consectetur a
eiusmod tempor incidunt ut labore et dol
Ut einim ad minim veniam, quis nostrud e
laboris nisi ut aliquip ex ea commodo con

18pt KORINNA

HEADLINE'S HERE

60 pt. KORINNA SHADOW L.C.

Verit in voluptate vel
illum dolore eu fugiat nulla pariatur. At verc
dignissum qui blandit est praesent luptat

8 pt RULE

Amolqui officia deserunt mollit ar
rereud facilis est er expedit c
ccacnt optio est congue nihil
cator s t amet, consectetur a
iasincidunt ut labore et dol
sintveniam, quis nostrud e
pteu ex ea commodo con
cenderit in voluptate ve
illum dolore eu fugiat nulla pariatur. At verc
dignissum qui blandit praesent luptatum
molestias excepteur sint occaecat cupida

TYPEWRITER BLOWN UP
BY PHOTOSTAT

SWIPED FROM
BOOKS
PUBLISHED BY
DOVER PRESS

Sin culpa t harumd dereud facilis est er expedit dis
conscient to factor tum poen legum odioq
neque pecun modut est neque nonor et ii
soluta nobis eligent optio congue nihil est
religuard cupiditat, quas nulla praid om u

ercend magistinvitat igitur vera ratio bene sanos as iust
Lorem ipsum dolor sit amet, consectetur a
eiusmod tempor incidunt ut labore et dol

Huge initial
in subhead:
overkill?

60 PT LUBALIN GRAPH BOLD
18 PT HELVETICA MEDIUM

Ut einim ad minim veniam, quis nostrud e
laboris nisi ut aliquip ex ea commodo con
irure dolor in reprehenderit in voluptate ve
illum dolore eu fugiat nulla pariatur. At ver
dignissum qui blandit est praesent luptat

6 pt RULE

36pt AVANT GARDE
GOTHIC BOLD

16 PT AVANT GARDE
EXTRALIGHT L.C.

rather unexpected

molestias excepteur sint occaecat cupida
sunt in culpa qui officia deserunt mollit ar
soluta nobis eligent optio est congue nihil

Graphic Idea Notebook

Charts

Why are statistics so boring?
Because the dignity of numbers paralyzes
the editor, who is terrified by possible
inaccuracies. That may well be an over-
reaction at times, but even if it is *not*,
why is it assumed that inventiveness
in technique precludes either dignity or
accuracy? Obviously it does nothing of
the sort, and that's the purpose of this
page. At right: a percentage protractor
of impeccable accuracy. Below: nine pies
produced by the protractor—each pie with a
different feel to it, each ''saying'' something
different, yet each perfectly accurate
in its mathematics. There are no how-to
notes under them. Let them
speak for themselves.

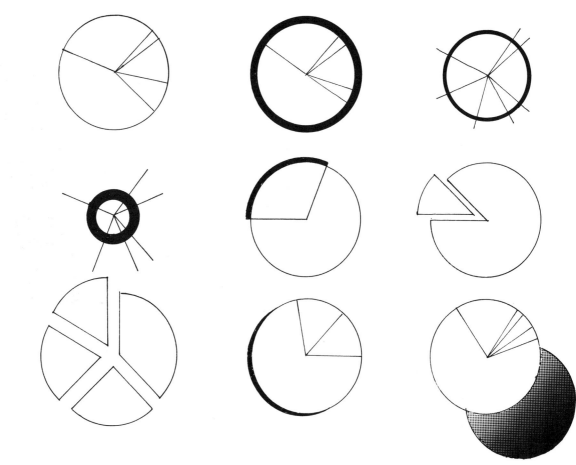

Embellish the pie with COLOR (if available) or with tints of the base color (black?). Tints are expressed as percentages, with 100% being "solid" ink, in increments of 10%. The printer will strip them in as specified, or do-it-yourself using the pressure-sensitive cut-out screens available in a bewildering variety of designs, textures and effects. But watch out for the labelling-problem: black words on dark blotchy backgrounds don't read too easily — nor do white ones on pale backgrounds!

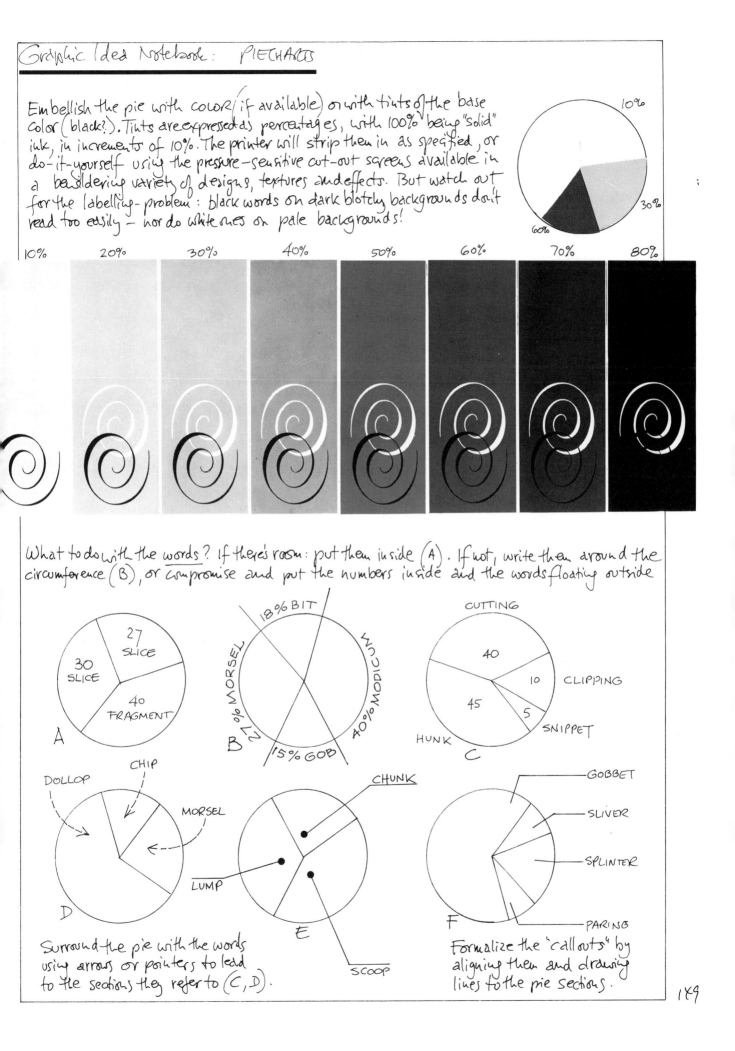

10%   20%   30%   40%   50%   60%   70%   80%

What to do with the words? If there's room: put them inside (A). If not, write them around the circumference (B), or compromise and put the numbers inside and the words floating outside

A
27 SLICE
30 SLICE
40 FRAGMENT

B
18% BIT
27% MORSEL
40% MODICUM
15% GOB

C
CUTTING
40
10 CLIPPING
45
5 SNIPPET
HUNK

D
DOLLOP
CHIP
MORSEL
LUMP

E
CHUNK
LUMP
SCOOP

F
GOBBET
SLIVER
SPLINTER
PARING

Surround the pie with the words using arrows or pointers to lead to the sections they refer to (C, D).

Formalize the "callouts" by aligning them and drawing lines to the pie sections.

149

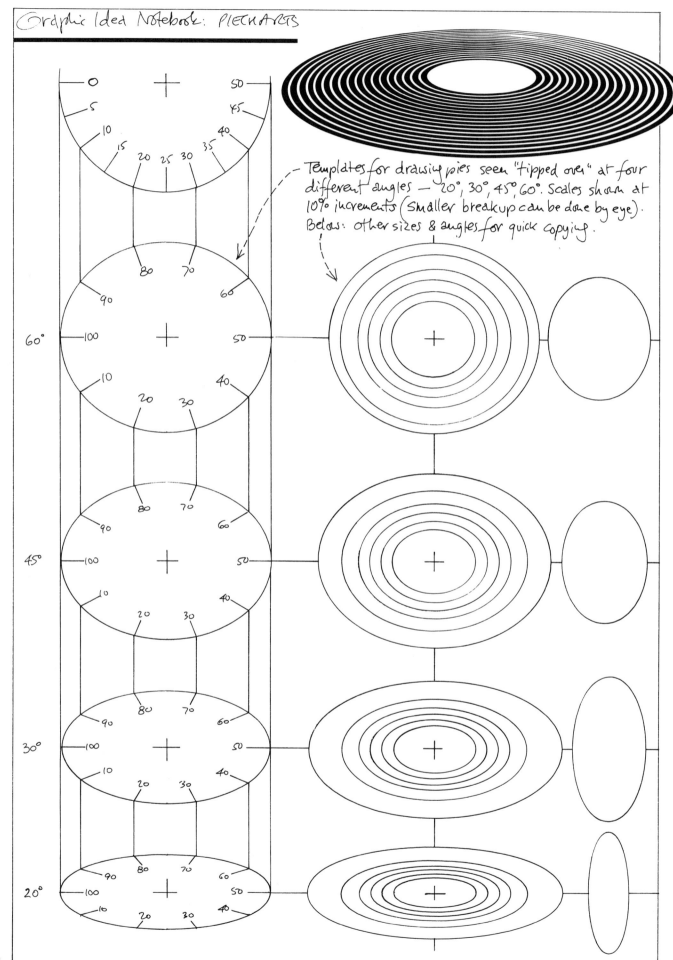

Templates for drawing pies seen "tipped over" at four different angles — 20°, 30°, 45°, 60°. Scales shown at 10% increments (smaller breakup can be done by eye). Below: other sizes & angles for quick copying.

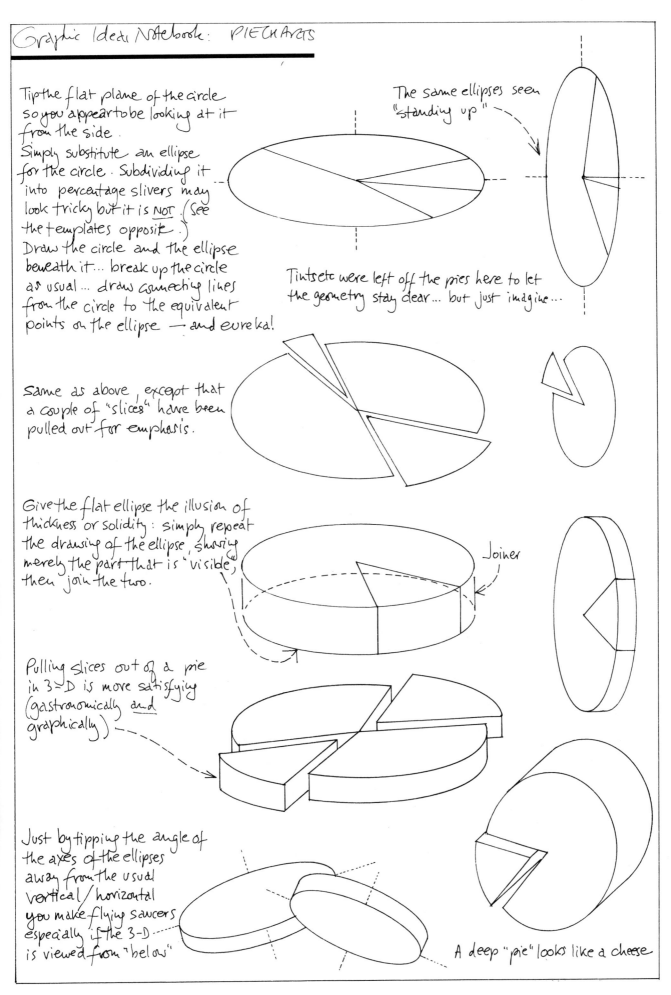

Tip the flat plane of the circle so you appear to be looking at it from the side.
Simply substitute an ellipse for the circle. Subdividing it into percentage slivers may look tricky but it is NOT. (See the templates opposite.)
Draw the circle and the ellipse beneath it... break up the circle as usual... draw connecting lines from the circle to the equivalent points on the ellipse — and eureka!

The same ellipses seen "standing up"

Tints etc were left off the pies here to let the geometry stay clear... but just imagine...

Same as above, except that a couple of "slices" have been pulled out for emphasis.

Give the flat ellipse the illusion of thickness or solidity: simply repeat the drawing of the ellipse, showing merely the part that is "visible", then join the two.

Joiner

Pulling slices out of a pie in 3-D is more satisfying (gastronomically and graphically)

Just by tipping the angle of the axes of the ellipses away from the usual vertical/horizontal you make flying saucers especially if the 3-D is viewed from "below"

A deep "pie" looks like a cheese

Work the piechart into the art in some way so that the statistics are illustrated, humanized, or made more palatable.

The chart is most startling if it can be shown as an INTEGRAL part of the illustration (like Behemoth's belly)

The piechart can be superimposed over existing artwork by dropping out the whole shape as → or by dropping out or surprinting the lines only, as ↓

The pie can be made out of a picture—here emphasized by a concentric screen

Make use of a circular object as the "base" of the pie-chart... a coin is the most obvious (and a cliché) but anything else of the right shape will do just as well — as long as it has something to do with the story.

Superimpose the slices in line over the halftone picture

or (better) cut the picture apart with the slices floating off in space ——→

View the object from an angle or lying down (NOT YOU! . IT!)

Cutting out the slice and having it float requires some tricky repair-work on the rest of the pie's edges, like here, where one edge is blackened for "shadow", the other just outlined and left white for "highlight"

More effective: paint the slices on a ping-pong ball and take a photo of the whole thing (with shadows!)

3.3%

If you show your pie as a solid sphere, indicating the slices becomes hard: the easiest is to superimpose them by stripping a black (or white) line over the picture.

To compare pies, use circular shapes of various kinds (e.g. Cones, balls, doughnuts etc).
Shadows yield an illusion of reality ... or floating above the surface of the page.
Use naturalistic images: apples, tires, doorknobs, hats, lightbulbs, kittens, pots ... name it.

A circle is not necessarily the only shape for a piechart, though it is the easiest to understand. Any shape symbolic of the WHOLE (- i.e. 100%) can be used just as well, but the proportions can be tricky: e.g. in the square, the radiating slices may be accurate in angle, but they are misleading in the areas they show. Vertical slices are more honest but this is no longer a pie - it is a CAKE... or bar-chart.

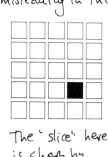

The "slice" here is shown by change in color

Breaking up the 100% into countable units

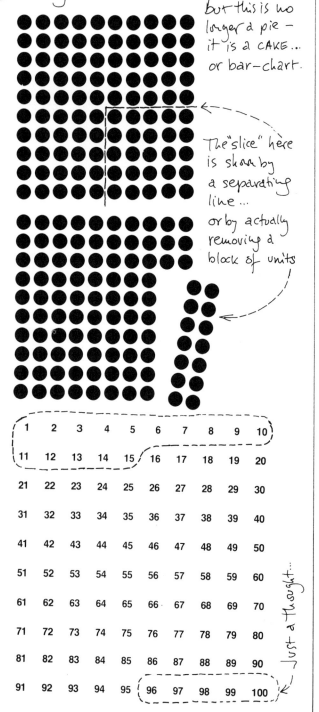

The "slice" here is shown by a separating line... or by actually removing a block of units

The 100% can be represented by a graphic symbol (3 versions of the Dollar shown here) which is then cut up in proportion to the statistics in some way. The effect is improved by 3-dimensional-illusion →

1	2	3	4	5	6	7	8	9	10
11	12	13	14	15	16	17	18	19	20
21	22	23	24	25	26	27	28	29	30
31	32	33	34	35	36	37	38	39	40
41	42	43	44	45	46	47	48	49	50
51	52	53	54	55	56	57	58	59	60
61	62	63	64	65	66	67	68	69	70
71	72	73	74	75	76	77	78	79	80
81	82	83	84	85	86	87	88	89	90
91	92	93	94	95	96	97	98	99	100

Just a thought...

154

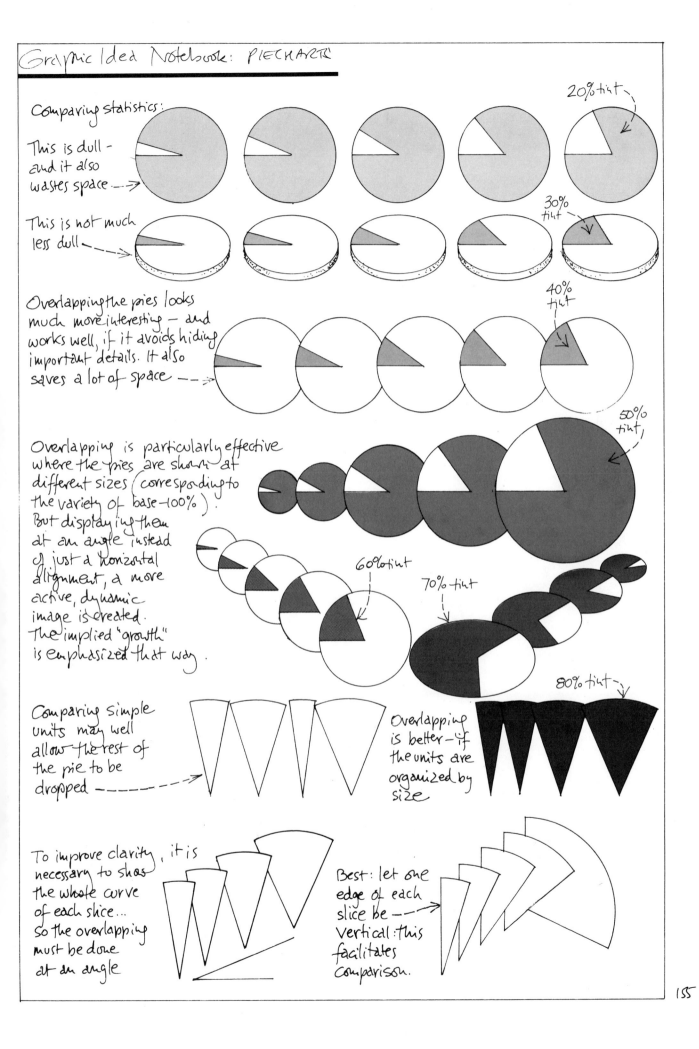

Comparing statistics:

This is dull — and it also wastes space →

20% tint

This is not much less dull →

30% tint

Overlapping the pies looks much more interesting — and works well, if it avoids hiding important details. It also saves a lot of space →

40% tint

Overlapping is particularly effective where the pies are shown at different sizes (corresponding to the variety of base-100%). But displaying them at an angle instead of just a horizontal alignment, a more active, dynamic image is created. The implied "growth" is emphasized that way.

50% tint

60% tint

70% tint

Comparing simple units may well allow the rest of the pie to be dropped →

Overlapping is better — if the units are organized by size

80% tint

To improve clarity, it is necessary to show the whole curve of each slice... So the overlapping must be done at an angle

Best: let one edge of each slice be → vertical: this facilitates comparison.

155

BARCHARTS

Charts are coming into their own. They are growing in usefulness because not only can they visually enrich a magazine, they also can act as vehicles for editorial comment.

Readers are accepting the fact that the scientific accuracy of statistics is not (necessarily) jeopardized if we make the graphics a bit more beguiling. So long as the numbers are plotted accurately, the magazine won't lose credibility.

Furthermore, editorial interpretation of or commentary on those statistics is becoming an increasingly acceptable technique. (True, some readers may condemn that as slanting—but let's not get into that one.)

Such editorial "interpretation" is achieved by the character of the draftsmanship, the exaggeration of scales, the addition of extraneous graphics, the symbolism utilized to turn ciphers into pictorial forms, and the context in which those pictorialized statistics is shown.

To simply "dress up" the raw material, all you have to do is handle the bars differently. (Handlebars?) Seventy-four variations on the basic theme will be shown to illustrate some of the ways. None of them are difficult.

To "interpret" the raw material, you have to work on the background against which the bars are seen; the commentary is in the context, not in the bars themselves. It is best to keep it that way, to avoid being accused of inaccuracies.

When you start combining the dressed-up bars from the following pages . . . with a spot of color, perhaps, if available . . . and with some interesting contextual treatment like the two below, you can see the limitless riches in this gold mine. Dig?

Editorial comment on statistics:
A.
The bars are placed in a background, where they become the focal points of the surrounding action or scenery. Easiest: someone holding them or pointing to them.

B.
The bars are part of the background and the action or graphic commentary is played out in the foreground

Graphic Idea Notebook — barcharts

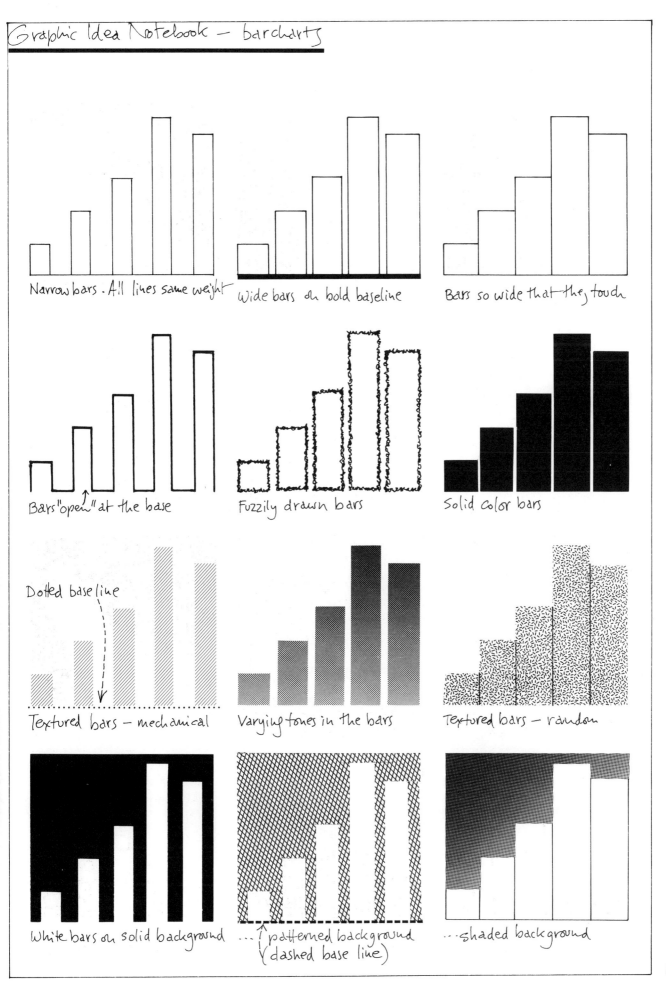

Narrow bars. All lines same weight

Wide bars on bold baseline

Bars so wide that they touch

Bars "open" at the base

Fuzzily drawn bars

Solid color bars

Dotted baseline

Textured bars — mechanical

Varying tones in the bars

Textured bars — random

White bars on solid background

...patterned background (dashed base line)

...shaded background

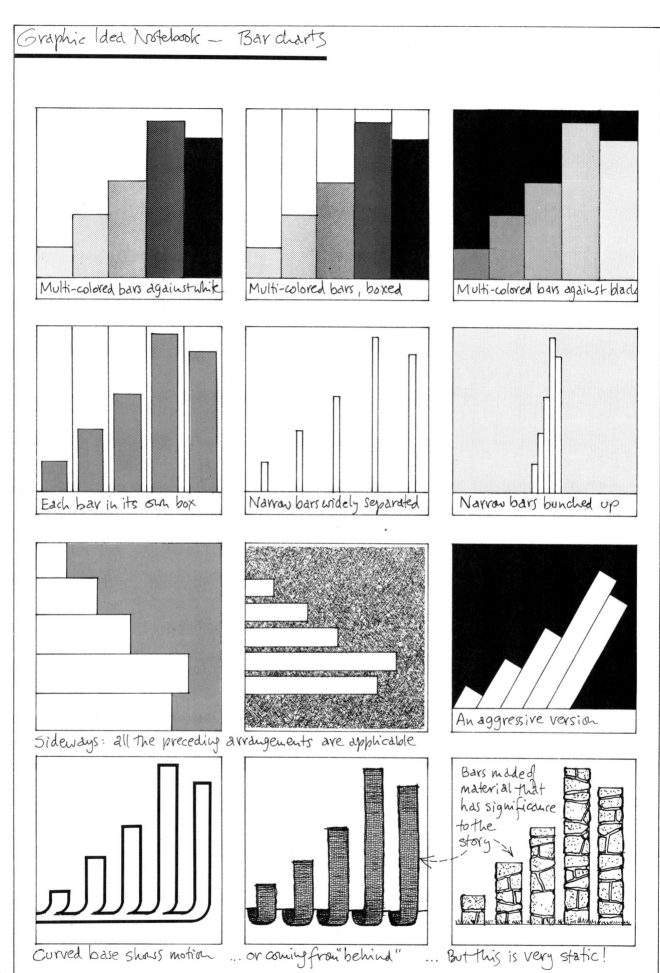

Multi-colored bars against white

Multi-colored bars, boxed

Multi-colored bars against black

Each bar in its own box

Narrow bars widely separated

Narrow bars bunched up

Sideways: all the preceding arrangements are applicable

An aggressive version

Curved base shows motion

...or coming from "behind"

Bars made of material that has significance to the story

...But this is very static!

Graphic Idea Notebook — Bar charts

Comparing 2 or more elements per bar:

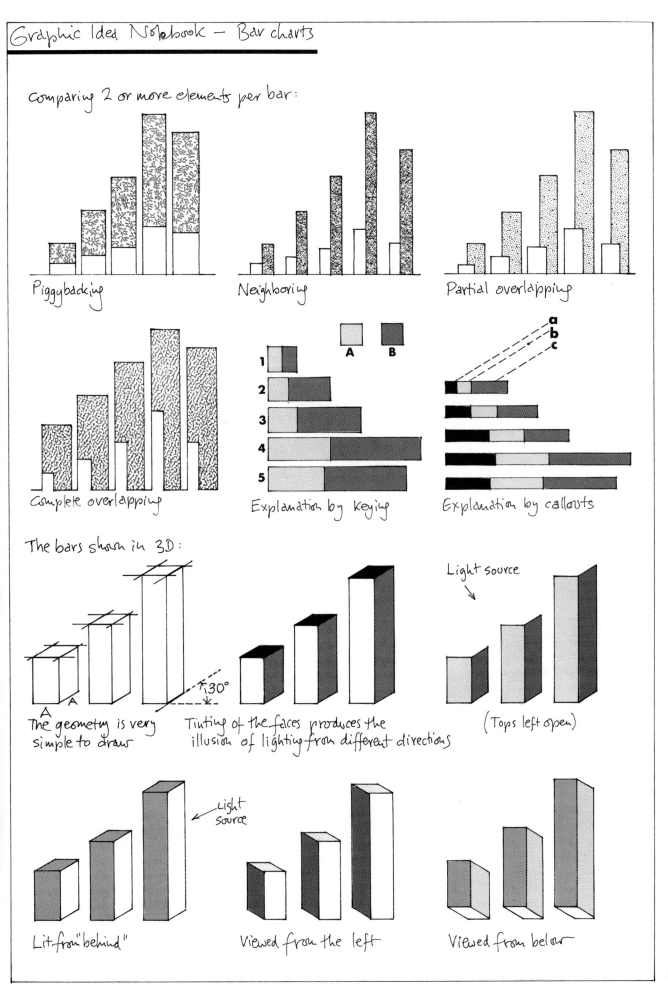

Piggybacking

Neighboring

Partial overlapping

Complete overlapping

Explanation by keying

A   B

1
2
3
4
5

Explanation by callouts

a
b
c

The bars shown in 3D:

A   A

The geometry is very simple to draw

Tinting of the faces produces the illusion of lighting from different directions

Light source

(Tops left open)

Lit from "behind"

Light source

Viewed from the left

Viewed from below

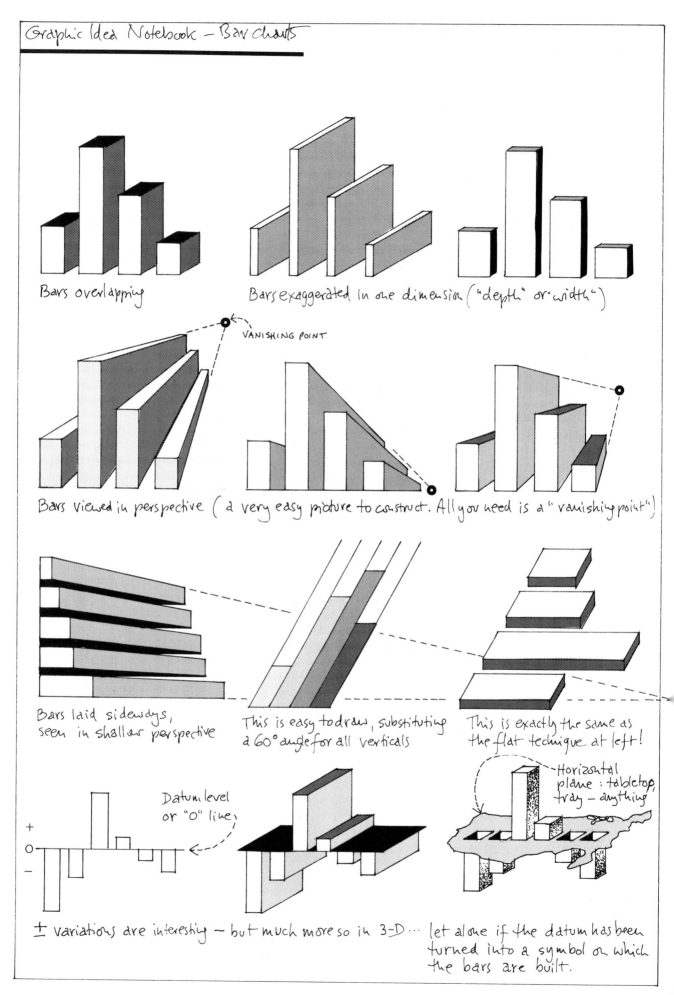

Bars overlapping

Bars exaggerated in one dimension ("depth" or "width")

VANISHING POINT

Bars viewed in perspective (a very easy picture to construct. All you need is a "vanishing point")

Bars laid sideways, seen in shallow perspective

This is easy to draw, substituting a 60° angle for all verticals

This is exactly the same as the flat technique at left!

Datum level or "0" line

+
0
−

Horizontal plane : tabletop, tray — anything

± variations are interesting — but much more so in 3-D ··· let alone if the datum has been turned into a symbol on which the bars are built.

Graphic Idea Notebook — Bar charts

What to do with the statistics

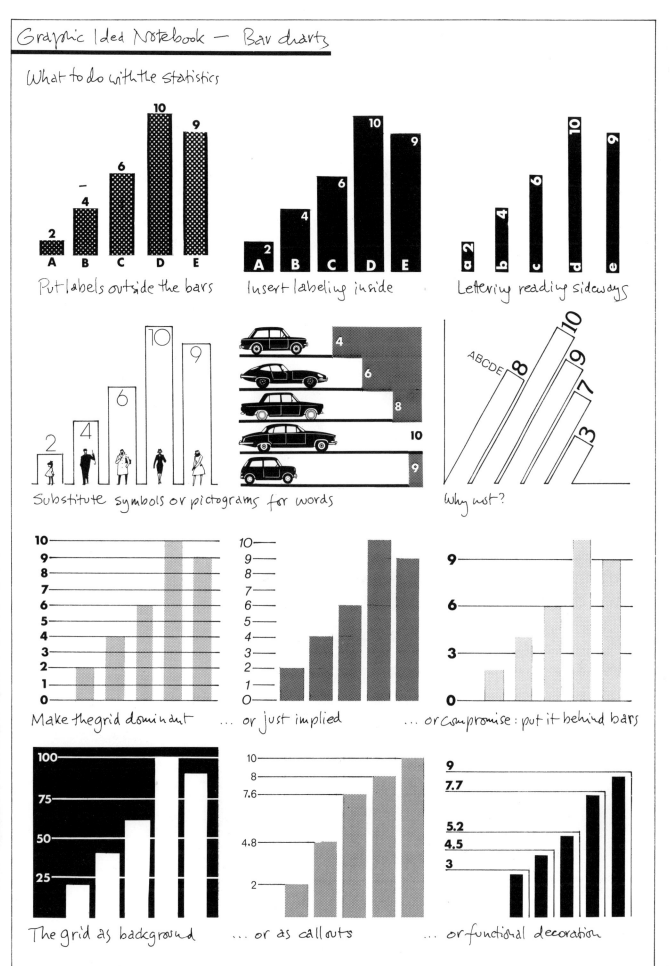

Put labels outside the bars

Insert labeling inside

Lettering reading sideways

Substitute symbols or pictograms for words

Why not?

Make the grid dominant

... or just implied

... or compromise: put it behind bars

The grid as background

... or as callouts

... or functional decoration

Graphic Idea Notebook — Bar charts

Who says that bars must be RECTANGULAR?

Drums…

…hexagons…

…triangles — all drawn with easy-to-use templates.

Dramatic geometry

Bars made of picture symbols … or "abstract symbols (countable)

Pictograms are easier to do in horizontal configurations

Substitute typographic symbols for pictograms

*E = [elephant]

EEEEE
EEE
EEEEEEEEE
EEEE
EEEEEE

How to subdivide a given length without a ruler that fits right:
1/ Mark off slightly bigger spaces on the edge of a piece of paper.
2/ Place the "0" in the corner of the chart, where the "0" will be.
3/ Pivot the paper on the "0" until the top number hits the top of the chart.
4/ Transfer the marks.
5/ Join to datum line.

Emphasize trends by joining bars with lines

Use realistic symbolism in photographs

* $E = Mc^2$?

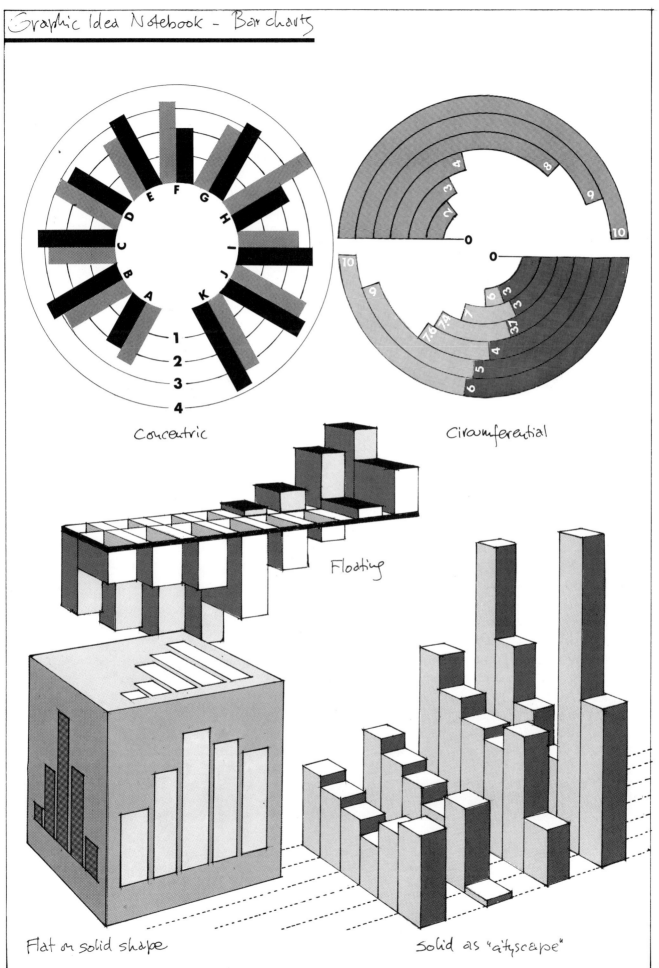

Graphic Idea Notebook - Bar charts

Concentric

Circumferential

Floating

Flat or solid shape

Solid as "cityscape"

GRAPHS

SCALE:
The interpretation of accurately-plotted statistics can be manipulated by altering the vertical and/or horizontal scales:

In these 3 simple graphs the figures are identical, yet the visual messages they send are very different:

This one is neutral ---
← This one indicates dramatic change
this one indicates sluggish change →

SIMPLICITY:
Where several lines are plotted together (BELOW) they must be widely separated to make each clearly distinguishable.
If, however, they create a spaghetti-like jumble they must be split apart into components

16 ⅞

THE GRAPH LINE:

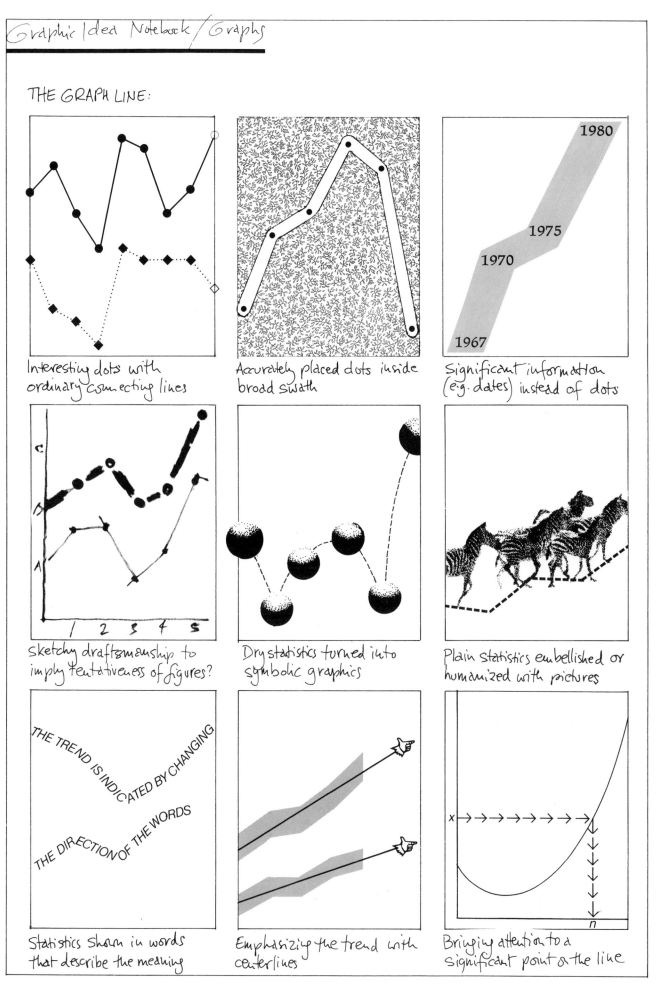

Interesting dots with ordinary connecting lines

Accurately placed dots inside broad swath

Significant information (e.g. dates) instead of dots

1980
1975
1970
1967

Sketchy draftsmanship to imply tentativeness of figures?

Dry statistics turned into symbolic graphics

Plain statistics embellished or humanized with pictures

THE TREND IS INDICATED BY CHANGING
THE DIRECTION OF THE WORDS

Statistics shown in words that describe the meaning

Emphasizing the trend with centerlines

Bringing attention to a significant point on the line

THE FIELD:

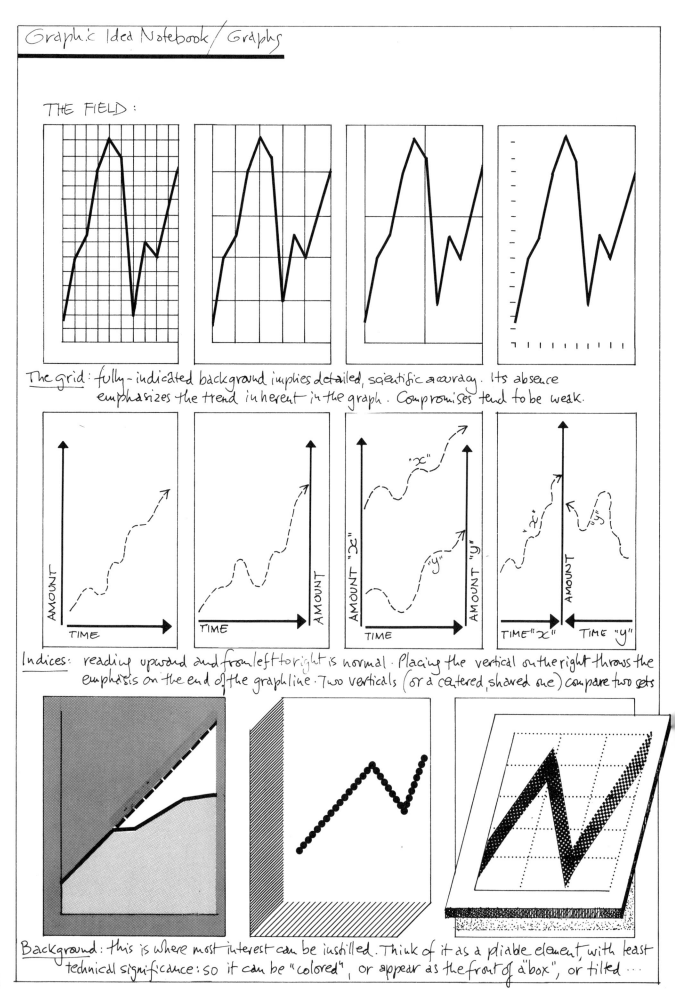

The grid: fully-indicated background implies detailed, scientific accuracy. Its absence emphasizes the trend inherent in the graph. Compromises tend to be weak.

Indices: reading upward and from left to right is normal. Placing the vertical on the right throws the emphasis on the end of the graphline. Two verticals (or a centered, shared one) compare two sets

Background: this is where most interest can be instilled. Think of it as a pliable element, with least technical significance: so it can be "colored", or appear as the front of a "box", or tilted...

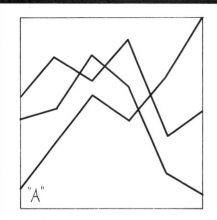

"A"

← How dull!   But here →
each line has its own weight:
the boldest is obviously the
most important and "nearest".

If the lines don't cross, it is much
more decorative to tint the
spaces between the lines:

↙ Here the tinting is random,
illogical — hence least successful.

↓ Here the progression is from

dark to light, whereas here ↗
it is from light to dark. This
is the least expected, thus it
is the most dramatic.

Combining a line with a
tinted background (be it
black on gray or white on gray)
is, perhaps the most effective
Compare these two with the
same statistics at top left ("A")

The simple mountain 3-dimensionalized

This is cheating, because it is obviously not completed at the ends

60°

Contrasting the mountain against the 100% seen beyond

Contrasting two mountains with the grid in between

Contrasting two mountains viewed from below

Three mountains seen as separated planes

Three mountains seen as butting planes in 3 grays

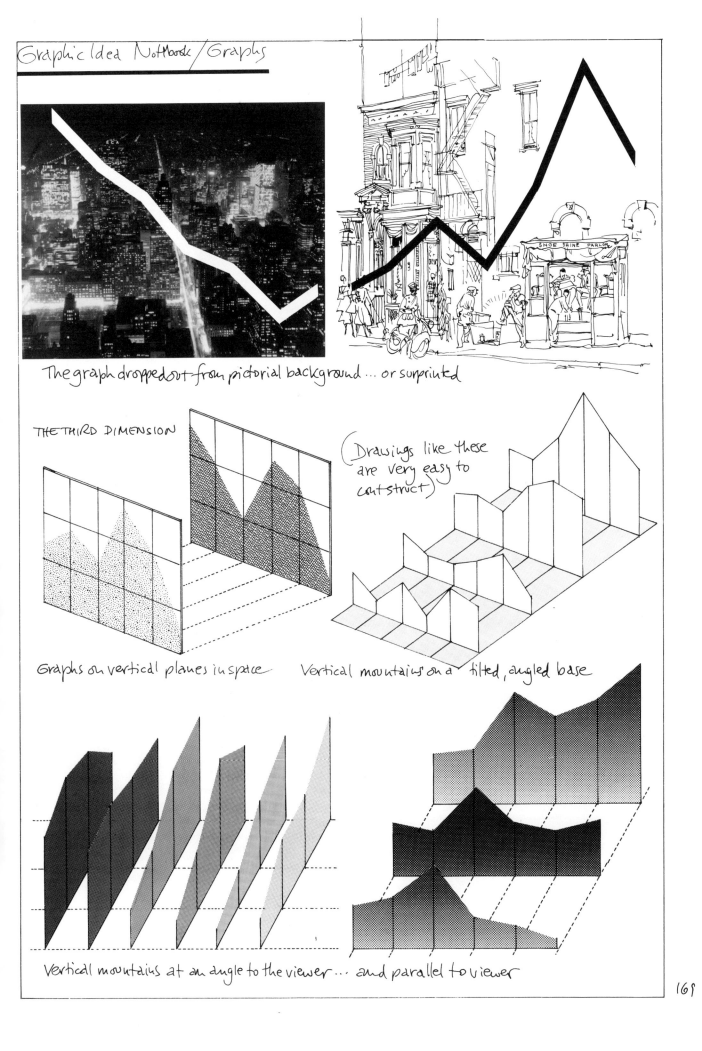

The graph dropped out from pictorial background ... or surprinted

THE THIRD DIMENSION

(Drawings like these are very easy to construct)

Graphs on vertical planes in space

Vertical mountains on a tilted, angled base

Vertical mountains at an angle to the viewer ... and parallel to viewer

The trends as ups and downs, leaving out all but the interrelationships. ← This is about as 3-D as one can get except for showing the steps disappearing to infinity →

Turning the graph into the central element of a symbolic pictorial scene.

Making the most of the surrounding frame: here are five typical patterns. Title can go up here

COMBINING CHARTS:

... as front planes on stacked boxes   ... as overlapping planes floating above the surface of the page

... as ends of square tubes in space

... as ends of stacked, staggered boxes

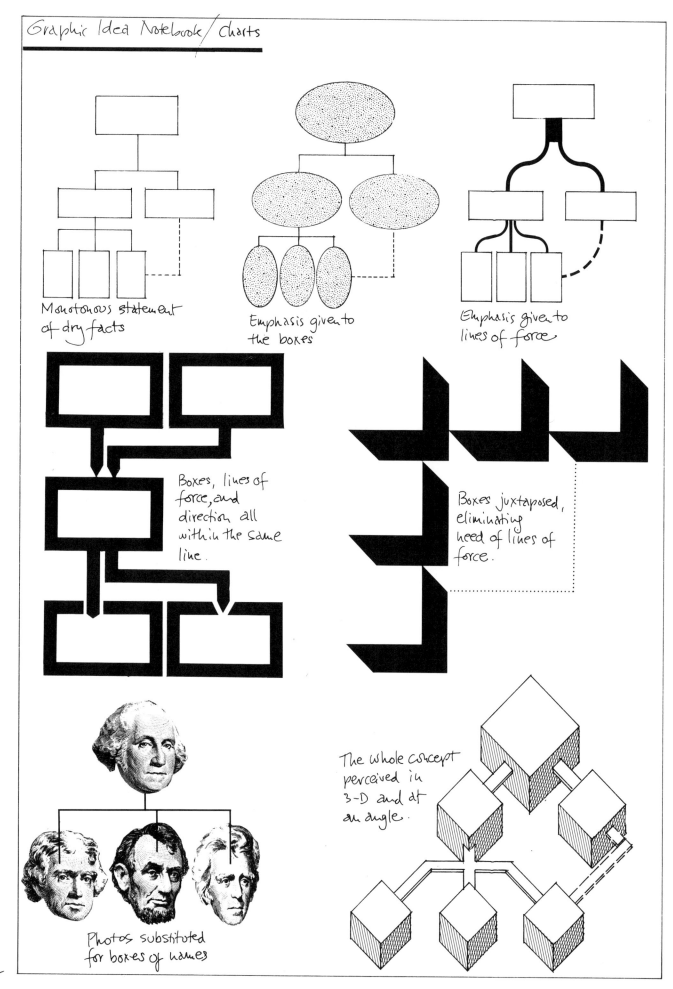

Monotonous statement of dry facts

Emphasis given to the boxes

Emphasis given to lines of force

Boxes, lines of force, and direction all within the same line.

Boxes juxtaposed, eliminating need of lines of force.

Photos substituted for boxes of names

The whole concept perceived in 3-D and at an angle.

Complicated relationships can be simplified by showing the focal points in 3-D and joining them with bridges at different levels. Overlapping can then look simple natural and understandable

Size of blocks and width of connectors can indicate degrees of importance

Height of walls shows comparative values

Boxes (drawn thus↑) or drawn in perspective can make a simple chart visually exciting

173

Maps

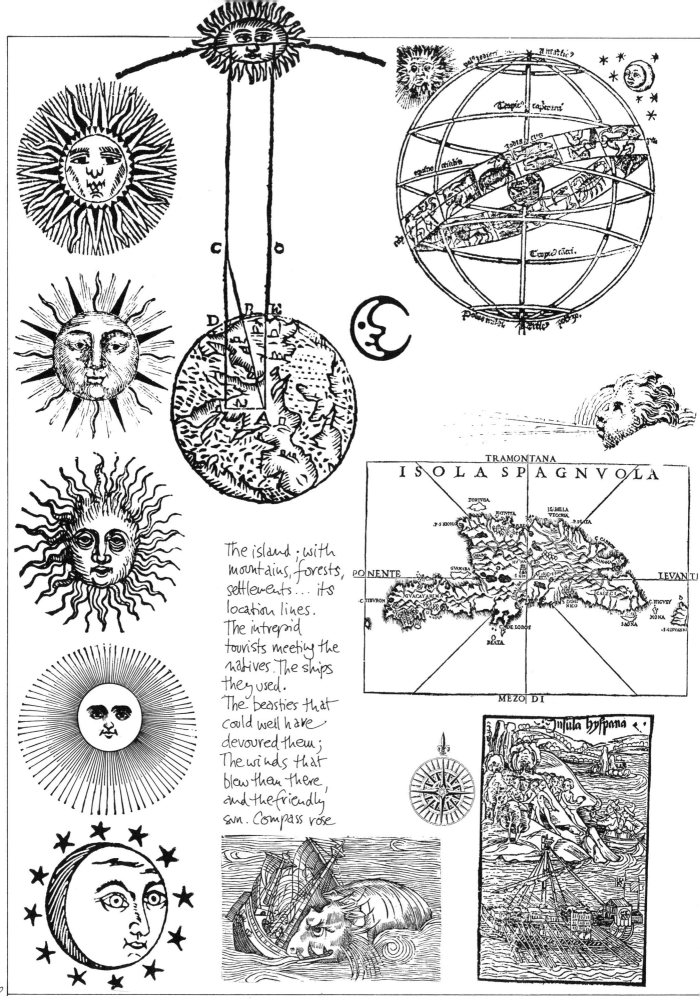

The island; with
mountains, forests,
settlements... its
location lines.
The intrepid
tourists meeting the
natives. The ships
they used.
The beasties that
could well have
devoured them;
The winds that
blew them there,
and the friendly
sun. Compass rose

MAPS

What is so fascinating about old maps? Well, for one thing, they are more than dry statements of where places are; they intrigue our imagination by telling a human story.

True, some of their charm also lies in their naivete, and there is no denying that we feel smugly superior in our sophisticated knowledge of the *real* facts. But they are documents created with infinite care and patience (and even humor) as well as awe at the responsibility for accuracy accepted by the cartographer. And, in addition, they are works of art.

By contrast, we tend to think of the modern map as cut-and-dried—automatic images, standard shape, size, outline; with north at the top, the sea in blue (or gray, if no color is available); and covered with names. Too little thinking goes into defining the message the map is intended to convey, for we think of a map as a sterile cliche only capable of showing the relation of one place to another. Yet the basic map can be manipulated graphically to do far more than just that.

Three examples of graphics utilized to accomplish different purposes:

1/ MAP AS PICTURE:
A naturalistic image of an area. Here, Alaska shown as a photo of a model with topography, colors & all.

2/ MAP AS DIAGRAM:
Plotting of places related to each other. Dot size represents size ... width of connecting arrows represents volume of flow between them.

3/ MAP AS GRAPH:
Areas built up of layers to indicate amounts — here: population of the boroughs of New York City.

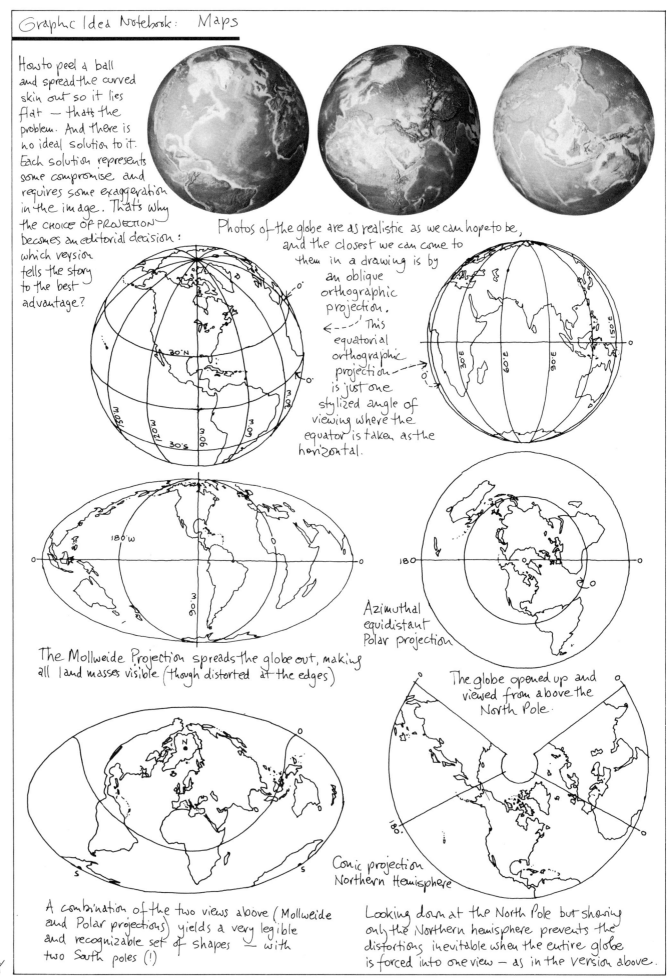

How to peel a ball and spread the curved skin out so it lies flat — that's the problem. And there is no ideal solution to it. Each solution represents some compromise and requires some exaggeration in the image. That's why the CHOICE OF PROJECTION becomes an editorial decision: which version tells the story to the best advantage?

Photos of the globe are as realistic as we can hope to be, and the closest we can come to them in a drawing is by an oblique orthographic projection.

This equatorial orthographic projection is just one stylized angle of viewing where the equator is taken as the horizontal.

The Mollweide Projection spreads the globe out, making all land masses visible (though distorted at the edges)

Azimuthal equidistant Polar projection

The globe opened up and viewed from above the North Pole.

Conic projection Northern Hemisphere

A combination of the two views above (Mollweide and Polar projections) yields a very legible and recognizable set of shapes — with two South poles (!)

Looking down at the North Pole but showing only the Northern hemisphere prevents the distortions inevitable when the entire globe is forced into one view — as in the version above.

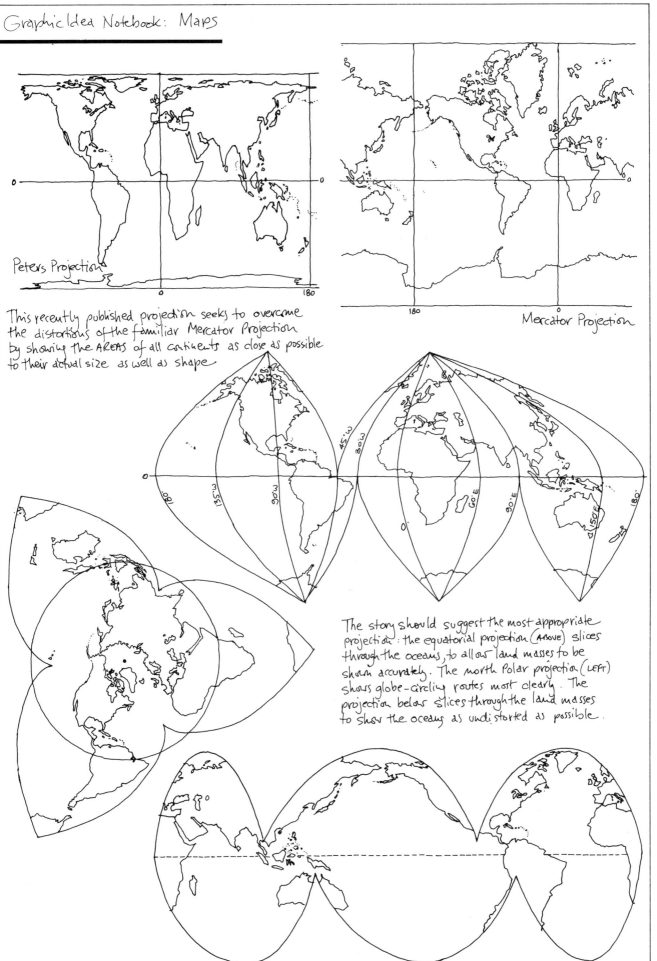

Peters Projection

Mercator Projection

This recently published projection seeks to overcome the distortions of the familiar Mercator Projection by showing the AREAS of all continents as close as possible to their actual size as well as shape.

The story should suggest the most appropriate projection: the equatorial projection (ABOVE) slices through the oceans, to allow land masses to be shown accurately. The north Polar projection (LEFT) shows globe-circling routes most clearly. The projection below slices through the land masses to show the oceans as undistorted as possible.

179

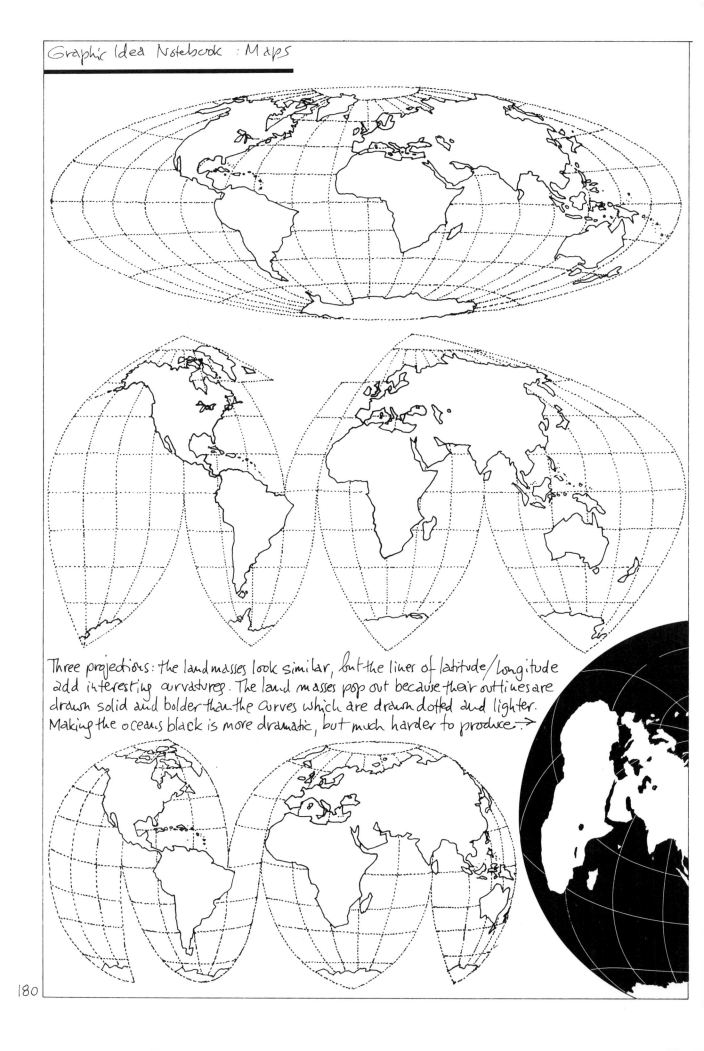

Three projections: the land masses look similar, but the lines of latitude/longitude add interesting curvatures. The land masses pop out because their outlines are drawn solid and bolder than the curves which are drawn dotted and lighter. Making the oceans black is more dramatic, but much harder to produce.→

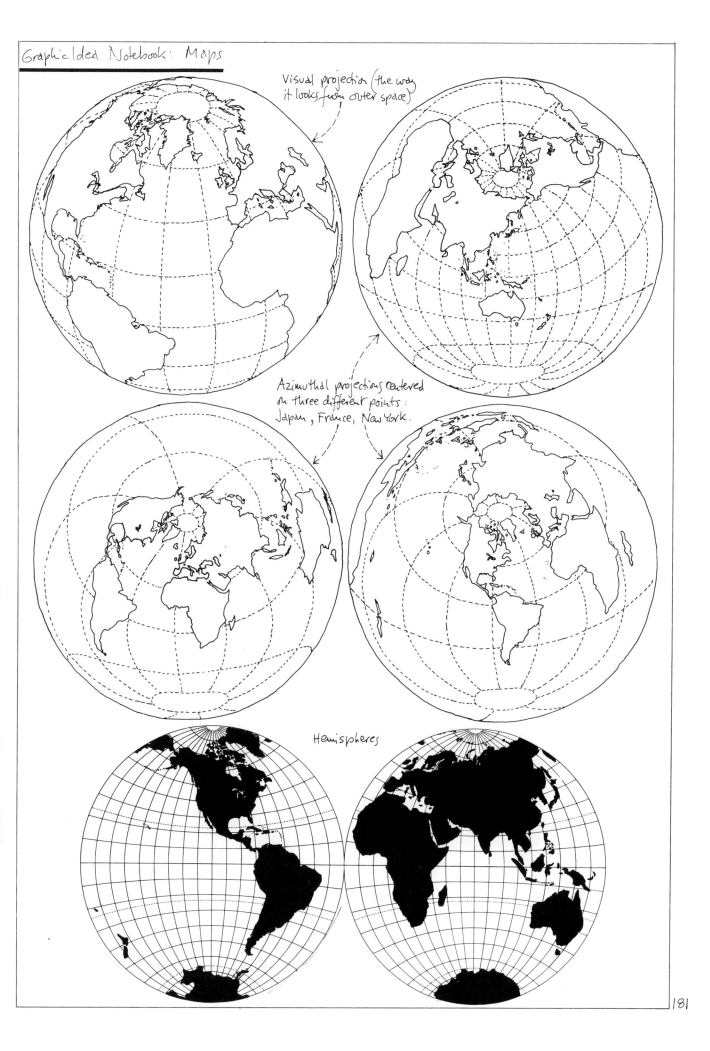

Visual projection (the way it looks from outer space)

Azimuthal projections centered on three different points: Japan, France, New York.

Hemispheres

Maps used for non-geographic purposes — as graphic images of statistical data.

Amounts indicated by "thickening" the areas.

Amounts indicated by changing the proportions of the parts in relation to each other:

Comparison of oil and gas reserves in various areas of the world.

Gross National Product indicated by "size" of country — contrasted to size of population

Stylized draftsmanship: using only verticals and horizontals ———— or basing the map on 45°.

Computer-drawn (much more dramatic as white lines on black)

The globe used for non-geographic purposes: as symbol, cartoon, decoration, interesting graphic spot, humorous subject etc

whizzing around →

hollow ---

cracked →

globe shape implied by place names written in concentric rings →

ANGMAGSSALIK · ZEEBUGG ·
SAUGATUCK · GUINCHO · KEEKOROK · ZAGOUAN · PUCKLE
MARSAXLOKK · SWAYAMBUNATH · ABERGAVENNY · IPI · CHURCH ·
'SGRAVENHAAG · MATMATA · CASTELLAMARE · PONTYPRIDD ·
HLEAKALA · ISCHL · BEEF · KIRKJUBÆ · RI · MZIMA ·
HREAT DOG · MONONGAHELA · PARK · KHAJURAHO ·
GMOUC · DO · ALBUQUERQUE · NITEROI ·
ORTQUE · AREMA · RANGA · NGORONGORO ·
CAIXAMBU · KALUSTUR · TEOTIHUACAN ·

pixielated inflated (c. 1904)

Toronto · Montreal
· Boston
· Calgary · New York
· Vancouver · Washington London
· Miami Lisbon

· San Francisco
· Los Angeles
· Guadalajara
· Mexico City
· Acapulco

· Lima
· Santiago
· Buenos Aires

Outlines of land masses omitted — yet the image of a globe retained by the correct (more or less) positioning of place names.

Paraphernalia ...
just a reminder of some of the symbolic resources that can be brought in when the editorial need arises. They can range from old cuts in the public domain, to cartooned versions of the same subjects....

and – taking other liberties with the material – why not make the globe the WRONG shape on purpose? Polyhedron? Better: draw it on an object like an apple, light bulb, stone, etc etc and then make a photo of it. Startling!

Beyond our globe:

← Atlas continues supporting the load he's carried since ±150 AD (now in New York's Metropolitan Museum) and shows Ptolemy's interpretation of the heavens. RIGHT: the latest in armillary spheres as of 1865. How about NASA's pictures of Spaceship Earth, or moonscapes – or ...

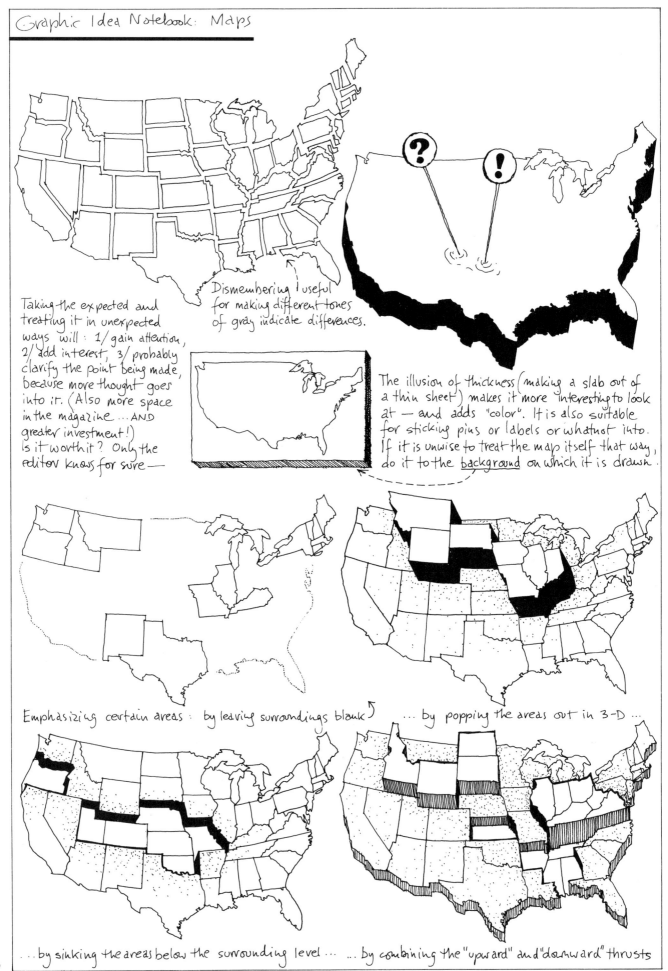

Dismembering' useful for making different tones of gray indicate differences.

Taking the expected and treating it in unexpected ways will: 1/ gain attention, 2/ add interest, 3/ probably clarify the point being made, because more thought goes into it. (Also more space in the magazine ... AND greater investment!) Is it worth it? Only the editor knows for sure —

The illusion of thickness (making a slab out of a thin sheet) makes it more interesting to look at — and adds "color". It is also suitable for sticking pins or labels or whatnot into. If it is unwise to treat the map itself that way, do it to the background on which it is drawn.

Emphasizing certain areas: by leaving surroundings blank↗ ... by popping the areas out in 3-D ...

...by sinking the areas below the surrounding level ... ... by combining the "upward" and "downward" thrusts

Graphic Idea Notebook: Maps

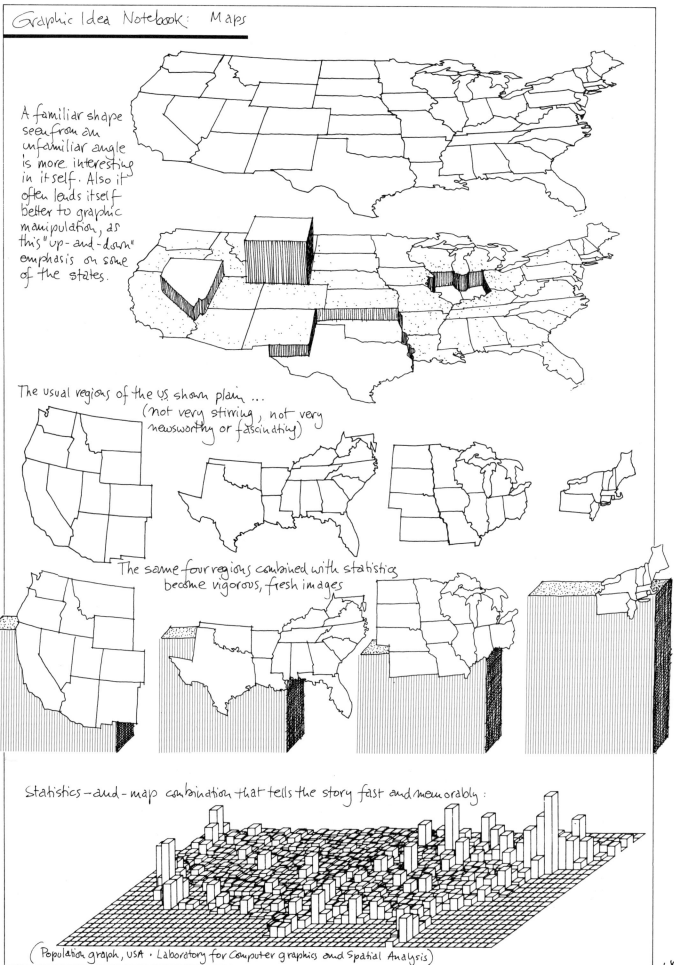

A familiar shape seen from an unfamiliar angle is more interesting in itself. Also it often lends itself better to graphic manipulation, as this "up-and-down" emphasis on some of the states.

The usual regions of the U.S. shown plain...
(not very stirring, not very newsworthy or fascinating)

The same four regions combined with statistics become vigorous, fresh images

Statistics-and-map combination that tells the story fast and memorably:

(Population graph, USA · Laboratory for Computer graphics and Spatial Analysis)

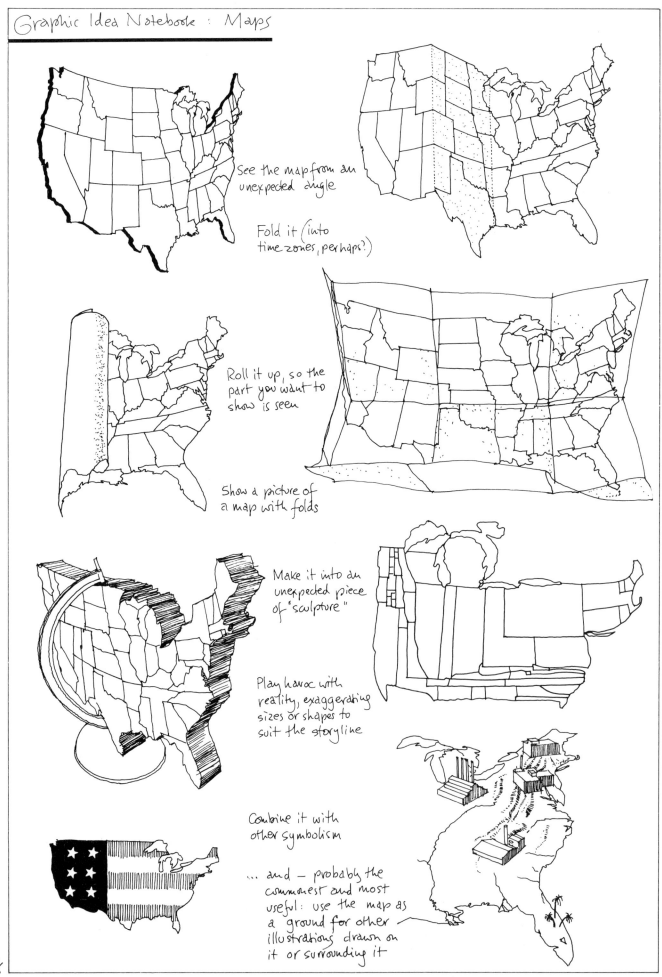

See the map from an unexpected angle

Fold it (into time zones, perhaps?)

Roll it up, so the part you want to show is seen

Show a picture of a map with folds

Make it into an unexpected piece of "sculpture"

Play havoc with reality, exaggerating sizes or shapes to suit the storyline

Combine it with other symbolism

... and — probably the commonest and most useful: use the map as a ground for other illustrations drawn on it or surrounding it

Instead of the ordinary, straight-down view, pretend you're flying in space, and are APPROACHING the area. Seeing it at a lower angle adds interest, and can be utilized to emphasize the editorial reason for which the map is being run.

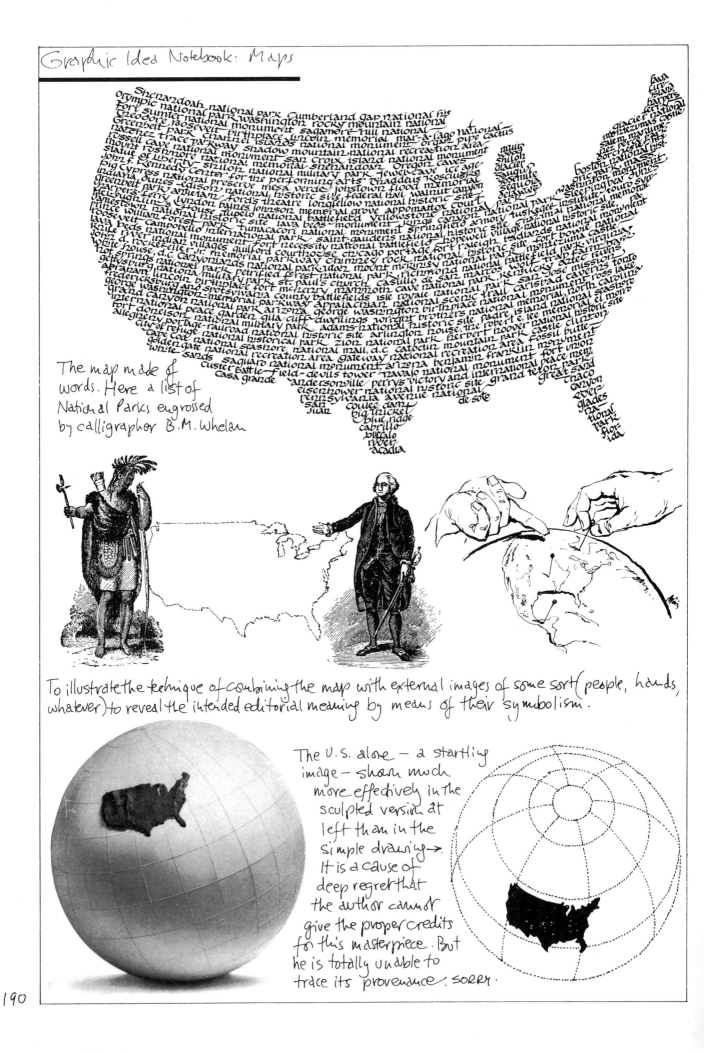

The map made of words. Here a list of National Parks engrossed by calligrapher B.M. Whelan

To illustrate the technique of combining the map with external images of some sort (people, hands, whatever) to reveal the intended editorial meaning by means of their symbolism.

The U.S. alone — a startling image — shown much more effectively in the sculpted version at left than in the simple drawing → It is a cause of deep regret that the author cannot give the proper credits for this masterpiece. But he is totally unable to trace its provenance. SORRY.

190

Cut the map out of unexpected
material. Here a reproduction
of sackcloth was used, and
the edges retouched with pen
and ink to simulate knots
(well-enough to fool the eye
at first glance, anyway):
Far more dramatic: to make
it of some REAL material
and then photograph it as
realistically as possible:
as a pie? a steak? a brick
walkway? plywood? carpeting?
Anything flat is possible to use.

Superimpose the shape over
a picture (here as a 40%
screen over an old steel
engraving)----

Silhouette a picture in the shape
of the map: here — obviously —
the idea is "Go west young man"